W9-CAZ-432

Testing Cloud Services

Kees Blokland has worked for Polteq as a senior test consultant since 2003 and has over twenty years experience in the testing profession. As the R&D manager, he has always been closely involved in testing innovations at Polteq. Kees is the first-line contact on cloud issues for customers and colleagues. He teaches many practical and theoretical courses in the field of testing and he is an experienced speaker on the national and international test stage.

Jeroen Mengerink has worked for Polteq since 2008 and is a test consultant. In addition to his work for customers, he is involved in various Polteq testing innovations. Jeroen is the first-line contact on Agile issues for colleagues and customers. He is a trainer for a diverse assortment of testing trainings, including the subjects of Agile, SOA and Cloud. He is also interested in the field of test automation.

Martin Pol has played a significant role in helping to raise the awareness and improve testing in Europe, Asia and the Americas, since 1983. He has gained experience by managing testing processes and implementing adequate testing in different branches of many organizations. He was responsible for the creation of international testing standards and models for test process improvement. Martin's extensive experience and knowledge formed the unique architectural foundation for the approach in this fine book.

Polteq is an independent provider of international software testing services based in The Netherlands and Belgium. Polteq testing professionals are requested to execute test assignments or to help solve testing issues worldwide. Polteq offers consultancy and training for testing cloud services under the commercial label Cloutest®.

Kees Blokland, Jeroen Mengerink, Martin Pol

Testing Cloud Services

How to Test SaaS, PaaS & IaaS

Kees Blokland, Jeroen Mengerink, Martin Pol

Editor: Dr. Michael Barabas/Maggie Yates
Copyeditor: Judy Flynn
Proofreader: Carey Hobart
Project Manager: Matthias Rossmanith
Layout: Josef Hegele
Cover Design: Helmut Kraus, www.exclam.de
Printer: Edwards Brothers Malloy
Printed in the USA

ISBN 978-1-937538-38-5

1st Edition
© 2013 by Rocky Nook Inc.

Rocky Nook Inc.
802 East Cota St., 3rd Floor
Santa Barbara, CA 93103

www.rockynook.com

Library of Congress Cataloging-in-Publication Data

Blokland, Kees, 1962-
 Testing cloud services : how to test SaaS, PaaS & IaaS / Kees Blokland, Jeroen Mengerink, Martin Pol. -- 1st
edition.
   pages cm
 ISBN 978-1-937538-38-5 (pbk.)
 1. Cloud computing. 2. Application software--Testing. I. Mengerink, Jeroen. II. Pol, Martin, 1947- III. Title.
 QA76.585.B56 2013
 004.67'82--dc23
                          2013022943

TOGA® and Cloutest® are registered trademarks of Polteq.

Distributed by O'Reilly Media
1005 Gravenstein Highway North
Sebastopol, CA 95472

Contents

Introduction from the CEO

I consider myself very lucky to be the executive lead of Polteq. The foundation of this company is a mix of experienced and young IT workers; the combination of doing, learning, improving and appreciating makes the cooperation a blast for the Polteq employees as well as for the customers.

Since it was founded in 2000, Polteq has always paid a lot of attention to the development of the test profession. A renowned test company like Polteq cannot, therefore, ignore the cloud. In 2008, the first steps were made to develop an approach for testing cloud services. Studies, experience, perseverance and a hefty R&D budget have resulted in a unique and, most of all, practical approach for testing applications in the uncertain digital cloud.

No one needs to invent the cloud-testing wheel anymore, since Kees Blokland, Jeroen Mengerink and Martin Pol have done that already, together with many colleagues.

This book will enable you to start right away and help you navigate the process of testing in the cloud. It is probably clear that we at Polteq, and me in particular, are thrilled to have reached this milestone. It may not surprise you that Polteq offers consultancy and training for testing cloud services. For that we chose the commercial label Cloutest®.

Alain Bultink
CEO Polteq Test Services BV

Preface

We all have heard about the cloud, even without knowing it. When you receive a link to download a file online for instance, you probably are already in the cloud. As a user you don't stop and think about the risks. What if, for instance, thousands of people simultaneously download this file? Can you accept the fact that this process will be extremely slow? Or when you send an email with your online client application, you very much would like it to be sent with the appropriate privacy. The entire world, of course, is able to access the cloud.

The term *cloud* comes from the fact that data packages no longer travel along a defined path. One doesn't know any longer by which path they reach their end point. We can no longer say for certain which route has been taken. This explanation contains a number of aspects that, as a tester, makes you think. "No defined path" and "no longer say for certain" are aspects that we as testers actually are not really looking for—quite the opposite. How can we make a statement about quality without having these certainties? Cloud computing has proven its use over the past years, and nobody doubts that anymore. But it quickly becomes clear that cloud computing brings a certain number of specific risks. As testers, we often say, "We can test everything!" But is this true? Are we really ready to test cloud computing applications?

And then I was asked by Kees, Jeroen, and Martin to write this preface. My first thought was, "Finally, a book on testing applications developed for the purpose of cloud computing." During conferences we gradually gained some information, but it still was a puzzle to create a complete approach. But we did, and that is exactly what you can find in this book. This book even goes further than the questions I originally had. It is also about how we can use cloud computing to execute our tests. It provides a very structured overview of what cloud computing actually is and how as a test manager you need to position your tasks.

This book is not revisiting the tasks within the testing profession. That is available in other literature. The approach of *Testing Cloud Services* mainly points to how you broaden your set of tasks as a tester and test manager within the context of cloud computing. Using checklists, tips, and examples, we receive all the information we need. Cloud computing has different risks on which we have to base our tests, such as manageability, continuity, and security. It is this shift in risks to which the testing world needs to act.

I am convinced that every reader of this book will discover useful aspects about testing of and with cloud computing. I am definitely going to apply this in practice; you need to also!

> Erik Boelen
> Test consultant
> qa consult
> Tongeren, Belgium, 9 February 2012

Acknowledgements

This book could not have been created without the input of quite a team of people. Our Polteq colleagues have spent many hours reviewing the content of this book. Their suggestions for improvement helped bring the quality of the book up to a level becoming of Polteq. The review team consisted of Anja Bakker, Danny Berrevoet, Jasper de Boer, Bjorn van den Brink, Jos van de Goede, Erwin Lamberts, Jeroen Lamberts, Hans van Loenhoud, Riny Nieuwhoff, Gerard Numan, Linda Pol, Susanne Spijkers, Marjolein Steyerberg, Ruud Teunissen, Wim ten Tusscher, Martijn de Vrieze and Douwe Wienke. Our colleague Arno Hofstra translated the Dutch book into English. Also, we are very grateful for the contributions of all our Polteq and non-Polteq "brothers-in-arms" that are not mentioned by name.

We are extremely pleased with the beautiful, artistic illustrations created by Lex Oosterman. His drawings introduce the major themes of the content in a subtle way.

Erik Boelen, from the Belgian testing community, is a good friend of Polteq. His striking preface is a compliment to this book.

We realize that it is a privilege to be able and to be allowed to write a book like this. That's why we are proud to be "Polteqers" and grateful to our families for giving us the room to do this!

Kees Blokland
Jeroen Mengerink
Martin Pol

1 Introduction

Cloud computing is a sea change in the way information systems are created and used. This simple fact is enough reason to investigate the phenomenon of cloud computing from a testing perspective. At the same time, it is useful to evaluate the testing profession from a cloud perspective because cloud computing offers interesting new options and solutions for a number of old bottlenecks.

More and more organizations are choosing to use services from the cloud. There are different reasons for this, but two come to mind immediately: new opportunities and cost reduction. An example of a new opportunity is worldwide access to data, at any time and with any device. And cost reduction occurs by:

- Sharing resources with other customers
- Service providers buying in resources on an extremely large scale and therefore at low cost and, on that basis, offering cheap services
- Customers not having to invest in resources (anymore)
- Customers not having to invest in spare capacity in order to accommodate peaks and growth
- Costs being predictable, giving customers improved control over expenditure

This book is written mainly from the customer's perspective. People involved in introducing a cloud product and keeping it operational will gain a lot of knowledge, especially from the sections about mapping risks and taking measures to reduce those risks as much as possible. Therefore, project managers, test managers, and people in other test roles will benefit from reading this book. However, it does not limit itself to cloud computing customers only. A supplier that is capable of taking on the viewpoints of customers is more able to offer successful services. By anticipating the risks a customer experiences, a test manager on the supplier side can achieve a competitive advantage for their company.

In this book, a complete approach is described for the testing of and testing with services in the cloud. Innovations in the test profession come together with existing techniques and approaches. *Testing Cloud Services* contains a lot of test measures that are applicable within, but also outside, the cloud context.

Before discussing the approach in detail, Chapter 2, "What is Cloud Computing?" offers a definition of cloud computing. Examples of generally available application services in the cloud are email (Gmail, Exchange service from the cloud), storage (Dropbox, iCloud), customer relationship management (Salesforce), and enterprise resource planning and office software (Google Docs, Office 365). More and more applications are being offered as services in the cloud. These services are built on a foundation of infrastructure and platforms (hosting and development environments). Large, well-known suppliers, such as Amazon, Force.com, Google, and Microsoft, also offer different infrastructures and platforms as a service.

In Chapter 3, "Role of the Test Manager," the test manager's duties are explained, including which traditional test management tasks are important in the context of cloud computing. In addition, cloud computing clearly adds new elements to the job of the test manager, such as risk management during the selection stage and supporting continuity in production. Also, the use of cloud computing in testing itself is expanding; this is described in section 3.3.

Chapter 4, "From Risk to Test," offers an extensive overview of the kinds of risks that are introduced when implementing cloud services, such as security and performance risks. Of particular interest here are the risks that are not, or only rarely, present in traditional development methods. For instance, think about risks in the area of legislation and regulations and a new phenomenon: elasticity. Test measures for risk reduction are described (aiding the elimination of risk). The extensive list of possible risks and the link to test measures are the basis of the approach in this book. When reading Chapter 4 you need to realize that not all risks are always present. Risk analysis will determine which risks are relevant and which measures are needed.

Finally, Chapter 5, "Test Measures," provides an explanation of different groups of measures that can be taken. Alongside completely new test measures, such as testing to ensure adherence to legislation and regulations and testing elasticity, better known test measures such as testing security and performance are described. The notion of "testing" has a wide meaning in Chapter 5. Dynamic testing is just one of the forms of test measure that is used. In addition, various forms of static testing are discussed, which include performing audits, listing requirements and measures, performing various checks, doing reviews and inspections on documents, and configuring and reading monitoring tools and logging. This widening of the testing focus is an existing trend that is continued in cloud computing.

2 What is Cloud Computing?

Cloud computing is a phenomenon that is, consciously or unconsciously, used already by many. It includes the use of resources over the Internet, without the user knowing where these resources are exactly. On a daily basis, websites that are placed in the cloud are visited. What about email providers? Who actually knows where their email is located exactly?

What explains the rise of cloud computing? More and more technological innovations are occurring. By combining some of these innovations, cloud computing came into being (see Figure 2–1). The one-of-a-kind, worldwide, broadband Internet makes it possible to disconnect the physical location of the computers and data from the desk of the customer. The underlying web technology is based on standards, which allows everybody to access their data at any time and from any place and with any device. In addition, virtualization makes it possible to create any kind of environment of any desired size. In this way, logical and physical infrastructure is disconnected, without the applications and users being aware of it. The rise of service-oriented architecture (SOA), where application services based on standard formats and standard protocols are offered, also has strongly contributed to cloud computing. Grid computing, where computers collaborate so that tasks can be distributed over the infrastructure, provides the cloud with its very large processor capacity, which is conceived as "infinite." A final important influence on cloud computing is the payment model that is used: pay per use. We know this model from the utility world, where invoices are based on the amount of water, electricity, or gas that is consumed.

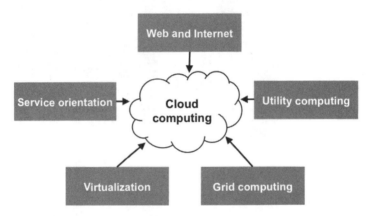

Figure 2–1   *Enablers of cloud computing*

With cloud computing, a world of new opportunities that can be fitted into the current IT landscape arise.

For a good understanding of the terms and concepts used in this book, a practical definition for cloud computing is essential. For this, we use the definition that is put forward by the American National Institute of Standards and Technology (NIST).

> **NIST definition of cloud computing**
>
> Cloud computing is a model for enabling ubiquitous, convenient, on-demand network access to a shared pool of configurable computing resources (e.g., networks, servers, storage, applications, and services) that can be rapidly provisioned and released with minimal management effort or service provider interaction. This cloud model is composed of five essential characteristics, three service models, and four deployment models.

The characteristics, service models, and deployment models (henceforth called implementation models) mentioned in the definition are separate dimensions of cloud computing that can occur in any combination. The risks that are described in this book are a direct result of one or more of the essential characteristics of cloud computing, the service model that is chosen, and the implementation model.

2.1 Essential characteristics

The five essential characteristics from the NIST definition are on-demand self-service, broad network access, resource pooling, rapid elasticity, and measured service.

On-demand self-service

Customers can configure computer facilities themselves, without human interaction with the service supplier. The services are easily available and can be obtained directly over the Internet.

Broad network access

Services are offered on a network. When standard protocols and standard formats are used, it is possible to obtain these services on different resources, such as PCs, laptops, tablets, and mobile phones.

Resource pooling

Multiple customers share the supplier's infrastructure through a rental model. The resources are appointed dynamically. This is done depending on demand from the customer. The exact location of the infrastructure is not important to the customer, though in general, the customer can set some preconditions, such as, for example, a particular country or a specific data center. The types of computer resources one has to think about—among others—are storage, computing capacity, memory, network bandwidth, and virtual environments.

Rapid elasticity

Services can be configured and released quickly and often automatically in an elastic fashion. This offers the capability of quickly scaling up and down. The customer experiences this as the apparently unlimited ability to obtain services at any moment and in any desired quantity.

Measured service

Systems check and optimize the use of the underlying infrastructure. Here, for example, the usage of the following is measured: storage capacity, computing capacity, bandwidth, and active user accounts. The result is transparent for the supplier and the customer and as a result is a fair basis on which to invoice.

2.2   Service models

NIST identifies three service models: Infrastructure as a Service (IaaS), Platform as a Service (PaaS), and Software as a Service (SaaS). Though on a regular basis new *aaS variants emerge, these three basic models suffice for a proper understanding of cloud computing. The service models form a service growth model, from IaaS through Paas to SaaS. Figure 2–2 illustrates a starting point of this growth model, where the following layers can be identified:

- **Hardware** is the equipment (servers, network resources, storage).
- **Virtualization** is the software that makes it possible to create multiple or different environments, based on the hardware. In fact, the software is running on an environment that is not physically present.
- **Platform** is a runtime environment in which software can run (.NET, PHP, Apache, etc.).
- **Application** is the software for the customer.

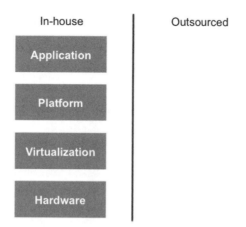

Figure 2–2   *No services purchased*

From the starting point in Figure 2–2, the first growth phase is the use of IaaS.

IaaS

The customer gets access to computing power, storage, networks, and other basic computer facilities and puts together their own infrastructure. The customer does not manage the cloud infrastructure but does decide which operating systems run on it, the amount of storage, and the applications that are rolled out on it. The customer also influences the configuration of network components such as firewalls. With IaaS, the hardware and virtualization move to the cloud Figure 2–3).

IaaS examples

Amazon and Rackspace deliver server capacity that can increase and decrease along with the needs of the customer. Companies get the opportunity to have flexible server and storage capacity without major investment. The pay-per-use model makes it possible to not have to make more expenditure than is strictly necessary.

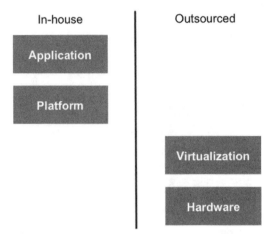

Figure 2–3   *Purchasing IaaS*

PaaS

With PaaS, the customer uses the programming languages and tools that are supported by the PaaS supplier. The customer has no control or management over the infrastructure but does have complete control over the applications and some of the configuration of the platform environment and makes their own choices for developing or buying them.

PaaS examples

Web hosting is a well-known form of PaaS. In addition to Hypertext Transfer Protocol (HTTP), web hosting companies provide an environment with a programming language such as PHP or Ruby-on-Rails and database options such as MySQL. This allows a personal website to be developed.

Windows Azure targets the development of cloud applications. A complete development environment is provided, where different programming languages can be chosen. Windows Azure is moving significantly beyond web hosting by providing development and test environments as well. And standard practice is to support a variety of resources such as various smartphones and tablets.

The customer therefore is not responsible (anymore) for the platform (see Figure 2–4). The examples show that there is a large diversity in the scope of the services (a stripped-down platform or a platform with an extensive development environment).

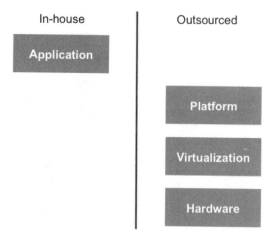

Figure 2–4   *Purchasing PaaS*

SaaS

With SaaS, the customer uses applications from a supplier that are running on cloud infrastructure. These applications are accessible through a simple interface—such as a web browser—for everybody, at any time, in any place, and with any device. The influence of the customer is limited to configuration such as the placing of corporate logos, language setups, and look-and-feel options. In this situation, all layers are outsourced (see Figure 2–5). In-house management remains only for the part of the IT infrastructure that is not moved to the cloud.

SaaS examples

Increasingly, webmail services like Gmail are used. The customers are used to having the service always available and from every location. They do not know where their mail is located and what the underlying infrastructure looks like, and in most cases, that is just fine. The customer has no need to perform any maintenance tasks, except on the emails themselves, of course.

Salesforce offers customers the capability of obtaining a customer relationship management (CRM) process from the cloud. The customer has access to all their customer data from any location. Like email, CRM is a clear and comprehensible process, so it can easily be offered as SaaS. Payment is done per user per month, keeping the costs clear and manageable. Through the scale of this SaaS form (development costs are indirectly shared by many customers), the customer gets access to a state-of-the-art facility without having to make a large investment.

In-house   Outsourced

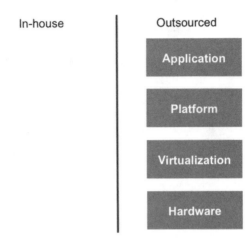

Figure 2–5   *Purchasing SaaS*

2.3   Implementation models

NIST distinguishes the following implementation models: private, community, public, and hybrid.

Private cloud

The cloud infrastructure is exclusively used by one customer. The cloud can be managed by the customer or by an external party and can be located in-house or in an external location. In practice, the difference between a private cloud and the data center of a large internationally operating company is limited.

Community cloud

The cloud infrastructure is shared by a number of customers and supports a specific community that has shared interests (such as security requirements, policies, standards). Management is done by the customers themselves or is outsourced. The infrastructure can be located in-house at one of the customer's premises or at an external location.

Public cloud

The cloud infrastructure is publicly accessible. The owner is the organization that provides the service.

Hybrid cloud

The hybrid cloud consists of two or more independently operating clouds (private, community, public) that are combined to make the exchange of data and applications possible.

3   Role of the Test Manager

The use and development of software continually changes, and that affects the activities and position of the test manager, as seen in projects where Agile methods are applied. The rise of cloud computing provides a new impetus to the role of the test manager. What is striking in Agile, as well as in cloud computing, is a shifting and broadening of focus. Managing functional software testing, originally the core of testing, is just one of the many tasks of the modern test manager. On one hand, this is because less and less traditional testing is done under the supervision of the test manager; instead it is done in Agile teams or by the service supplier. On the other hand, it is because nonfunctional requirements are claiming an increasing role. A documented test basis (requirements and specifications) is no longer the starting point for testing. The test manager increasingly bases measures on the desires and needs of the operation and users.

Thus, the test manager, as it were, climbs in the V-model and gets a broader responsibility: a process is successful when the business process and the users are supported properly.

Testing Cloud Services gives substance to this broadening of the role and offers test managers plenty of room to further develop themselves in the testing profession. The test manager, for instance, needs to be involved during the selection of services. In this stage, it becomes clear which requirements can be met and which cannot be met. After making a choice, one is stuck with the quality and options of the selected services, and their accompanying risks. However, this is not completely new: selecting a service is similar to selecting software packages. Here the test manager also provides a valuable contribution to the selection process.

The involvement of the test manager in the production phase is entering a new stage with cloud computing. In an IT landscape of connected systems, an increasing need for continuous system integration emerges. This is comparable to continuous component integration, where regularly (often daily) a new software build is compiled. An automated regression test in this case needs to ensure the continuity of the development process. With continuous system integration, something similar is going on: systems in production are updated all the time (patches, upgrades, new releases), which requires a more or less permanent regressive system integration test to ensure continuity in production. Where there is knowledge of the exact changes to the customer's own software, in cloud computing the customer can be confronted with unannounced and hardly documented changes. The continuous system integration test will be necessary as a backstop. The situation might even arise in production that makes choosing another service or service supplier necessary—for example, because testing shows that guarantees in continuity are not met.

In addition to a role during service selection and in production, there is a job that needs to be done during service implementation. This is like the traditional role of the test manager: testing and giving advice on getting information systems into production (operation). All in all, the role of the test manager has broadened (see Figure 3–1).

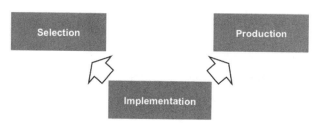

Figure 3–1 *Broader role of the test manager*

Cloud computing not only poses challenges for testing, it also provides interesting new testing options. For example, cloud computing can be used for test environments or test tools. It can also mean that all test activities and the test organization as a whole are brought to the cloud. This will be called Testing as a Service.

3.1 In general

Sufficient information can be found in the existing testing literature about the general tasks of the test manager. To support the test manager who is going to work in the cloud, in this section we'll describe the following activities:

- Risk analysis
- Reaching agreements on testing with suppliers
- Setting up and executing the end-to-end testing
- Giving advice

3.1.1 Risk analysis

No risk, no test. This remains the starting point for the activities that are executed by the test manager, no matter what. Test effort is on the cost side of the testing business case; risks covered (and with that, costs saved on problems in production) are on the revenue side. A risk analysis always forms the basis of the measures to be taken by the test manager. Chapter 4 provides many pointers to ways to mitigate many kinds of risks. A connection is also made to the choice of the characteristics, service, and implementation models of cloud computing. The test measures referred to in Chapter 4 consequently provide the building blocks for a test strategy. Because of the broader role of the test manager, there are measures that can be taken during selection and measures that can be addressed only during implementation and in production.

A (product) risk analysis is part of the standard arsenal of the test manager (see Table 3–1). With different stakeholders, the chance of something going wrong with the information system (in this case a service-based solution) is discussed along with the impact this can have. A large likelihood of failure with significant consequences represents a high risk and requires a lot of test effort. On the other hand, one should not make a big deal of testing an aspect with a low likelihood of failure with small impact.

Table 3–1 *Example of a risk analysis table*

System component	Risk group	Risk	Classification		
			Failure rate	**Impact**	**Risk category**
	Security				
	Performance				
	Manageability				
	Legislation and regulation				

First it is necessary to create an overview of the risks. It is important to involve people in this process who have a good view on what can go wrong when going to the cloud and people who can translate that to the impact of things that go wrong.

Next the risks are determined to a sufficient level of detail. Traditional product risk analysis techniques can easily be applied here. How does this work? For starters, with a team of people, the risks are worked out in more detail—for instance, what functionality can be distinguished and which security aspects?

For functionality, a division can be made based on the different business processes. To do this, an experienced user provides input. For security, the help of a more technically oriented person is needed. To determine the impact of failure, a translation needs to be made to practical situations: How high are the costs of fixes? Loss of revenues? How long can no invoices be sent? And so on. Based on the detail risk analysis, the test manager determines a test strategy in which large risks are allotted more test effort and small risks less effort.

In the testing literature, extensive attention is paid to the process of product risk analysis and using it to develop a test strategy.

3.1.2   Information from and agreement with the supplier

After the selection phase, implementation and production follow. In these stages, a lot of testing activities are deployed for which information and support from the supplier is needed. Think about service specifications (test basis), test environments, and guidelines for logging issues. When the supplier's standard terms and conditions do not fully provide them, additional agreement is needed with the supplier. The test manager needs to check the terms and conditions and ensure that the desired contract is drawn up. This is, however, not always a possibility because, for example, large service suppliers might not modify their terms and conditions for small customers.

Checklist for general supplier conditions and other sources

The test manager needs to, when applicable, watch for the following:

- Where can the interface specifications be found?
- Where can manuals be found?
- How are issues logged?
- How is the customer kept informed about the progress of the resolution of logged issues?
- What guarantees are provided for the speed of resolving (severe) issues?
- What are the guarantees on availability (including metrics agreements)?
- What are the guarantees on performance (including metrics agreements)?
- What are the guarantees on security (including metrics agreements)?
- Are there test environments available and how can they be used?
- How is the customer informed about changes in the service?
- How is the customer informed about changes in documentation?

- How is the customer informed about the test results of changes in the service?
- How can monitoring and logging facilities be configured?

Additional terms and conditions

Additional agreements may be needed based on inadequately answered questions from the checklist. There are aspects that are never standardized, such as agreement on the customization of the service or the interfaces to the service. Here are several other examples of issues to be addressed:

- Periodic supplier evaluations and reviews of service (for example, to what extent the supplier has met the guarantees on performance and other aspects)
- Mock services provided by the supplier
- Performing audits at the supplier (on security or process quality)
- Support with implementing the service

Try to avoid enforcing everything in a legal contract: the customer benefits more from a correctly functioning service than from penalty clauses.

3.1.3   End-to-end testing

End-to-end testing (E2E) is a profession in its own right. The notion of an E2E test is quite similar to the notion of process testing. This is sometimes referred to as the technical process or the system integration test, which is no more than a system test of more than one system. With the E2E test, the business process is foremost. The E2E test is therefore the broadest possible test, in which the end results are taken as a starting point. That the system integration test and the E2E test are similar may be obvious. The difference is in the focus and is determined by the risk that processes are not sufficiently supported. This risk becomes larger when the organization, the infrastructure, and the processes are more complex: who will be able to oversee and assess the cohesion between processes, functionality, and the technical infrastructure? It may be obvious that the E2E test is even more important in cloud computing and simultaneously increases in complexity (see Figure 3–2).

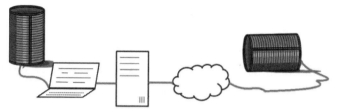

Figure 3–2   *End-to-end test*

E2E testing is more than system integration

System integration mainly focuses on interfaces between systems. Successful system integration is a necessary precondition for the E2E test because systems need to exchange information. The E2E test, in turn, tests the total combination of systems and business processes.

There are some surprises that can arise here:

- Inconsistent data (people with different addresses in different systems)
- Wrong (human) interpretation of data (what date is meant by 8-9-10)
- Data that is mandatory in one case and not in another
- Timing and order problems (messages processed in the wrong order)

The E2E test is not limited to functionality. Many nonfunctional properties of services need to be assessed in an E2E test environment, such as performance and security. The E2E test results therefore play an important part in acceptance of the service in the context of the IT landscape and business processes of the customer. Executing the E2E test provides an important spin-off: the knowledge gained is an important input for describing and testing the work processes and all accompanying documentation.

The focus of the E2E test

The focus of the E2E test is one with multiple dimensions. The first is formed by the business processes that use the IT landscape and in principle does not pay attention to how functionality is divided over different systems and services. These business processes form the most important basis for what needs to be tested. The second dimension is the so-called system picture: the systems and services are connected in a specific way, indicating information flows. Implicitly, this also includes the interfaces. This is the physical world in which the tests need to be run. The third dimension is the exact functioning of the systems and services in the IT landscape.

In preparing the E2E test, knowledge is needed of all three dimensions. This requires input from different functions: testers, technical experts (such as operators), and subject matter experts (for instance, users).

Creating E2E test cases

In section 5.6, a number of techniques are described to put together the test basis and thereby create a starting point from which to develop test cases. This process has to be done in close cooperation with subject matter experts: the business process is quite often not very well documented and can be hard for outsiders to understand.

Working out the logical test cases (for instance, from a classification tree) to physical test cases is quite a job, and the system picture, as well as knowledge of functionality detail, is needed. The steps are as follows:

- Describe all test actions in the E2E test case. For example, a test case starts in a certain system and after passing through a number of systems and services ends in another system with a certain result.
- Determine the data that represents the test case (for instance, values from the classes in the classification tree) and the expected result of the E2E test case.
- Determine the configurations and base data needed in all systems and services through which the E2E test case passes.
- Describe the expected intermediate results of the test case on all interfaces between the systems and services.

Executing E2E test cases

After an intake on the test environment, test data, and the versions of all systems and services has been performed, the test cases can be executed. This sounds easier than it is. A number of typical E2E bottlenecks can occur during test execution:

- The execution requires a lot of time (for instance, the business process requires that the next step is performed a day later).
- Running out of test data. When test cases get stuck along the way, the original data cannot be used again and resetting across multiple systems is very hard to do (a reason to create backup test cases).

- The test systems are not all available in time (when this is known in time, stubs/drivers or simulators can be deployed).
- Analyzing an issue is difficult (in what system or which service does the issue occur?) and requires a technical view and access to log files.
- It's not always possible to have the right people available to execute the test actions and to analyze the results.
- The supplier is hard to reach for answers to questions.
- Nobody has detailed knowledge of all systems.

Automating the E2E test execution

Fully automating the test execution makes effective and continuous system integration possible, but in practice, it is not feasible for many. However, there are many aids that can make testing in an E2E setting easier. For example, there are tools to generate test data, tools to generate messages and to analyze them, and tools that can function as stubs/drivers or simulators. Proper interface specifications are especially important for the correct use of all these tools.

E2E regression testing

In several places in this book, E2E testing is used as a regression test measure to test the impact of changes. The scope of the E2E regression test is connected to the risks to be covered. With every change, an E2E regression test is needed. The customer is, however, not always informed by the supplier on changes in the service. To detect the impact of unannounced changes in a timely fashion, the E2E regression test needs to be executed with an increased frequency. Because of this higher frequency, automation cannot be avoided.

Finding the cause of an issue

When the result of a test is not according to expectations, a well-documented issue needs to be logged. With part of the technical infrastructure in the cloud, analyzing problems is more difficult than when the software is running on the customer's own resources. A specialist cannot just run to the server room, because it is virtual and is "somewhere" in the cloud. For each issue, it is important to determine in which component the problem lies: in the (virtual) environment, in the platform, and so on.

Reading log files is one of the means that can be reverted to in such a case. Logging data needs to be configured in strategic locations in the E2E process to enable determination of where an error occurs.

3.1.4 Advice

The test manager determines the quality of the tested service. This is done in the context of the interfacing systems and the business processes and provides as good a picture of the remaining risks as possible. This forms the basis for release advice and is important information for the go/no-go decision.

Within the selection process, a clear moment emerges in which the advice of the test manager is needed: the decision for selecting a certain service (and a service supplier). The test manager needs to have the advice ready in time and has to know who the stakeholders are. A universal guideline cannot be given, but often a purchasing department has the lead in selecting IT resources. The task of the test manager during selection is finished when a deliberated decision has been made about a certain service, partially based on the information delivered on quality and risks.

After selection, an implementation process follows where configuration and testing processes occur. In the same way as when the customer's software is implemented in production, the test manager will provide release advice for the implementation of services. In this case, it is about the decision to bring a service into production. This seems similar to traditional test processes, where a board takes the decision to go live, partially based on the advice from the test manager.

When a problem is detected during the continuous E2E test—for example, after testing an update—the test manager needs to inform the organization and someone needs to decide on remedial measures. This can be implementing a workaround, rolling back the changes, or even choosing another service. In practice, it can be quite difficult to find the responsible person(s). In larger organizations there are often different system owners, and with cloud computing, sometimes an inaccessible supplier is added to the equation.

3.2 Tasks during selection, implementation, and production

3.2.1 Selection

Determining the suitability of a service is done based on selection criteria, and the cloud-specific aspects need to be emphasized. The fact that selecting a service implicitly or explicitly means a supplier is also selected, which is an important aspect here too.

Here is a step-by-step plan for the test manager:

1. Put forward cloud-related aspects
2. Determine completeness and controllability of the selection criteria
3. Assess services and suppliers
4. Issue a selection advice

For the first step, consult Chapter 4. The second step is similar to a test basis intake: is it complete and testable? Some test measures addressing the risks can be put in place during the selection phase. The test manager in turn offers advice based on the results of the test measures. Section 5.1 details the activities.

3.2.2 Implementation

Implementation encompasses all activities that are needed to take the service into production. From the risk analysis it becomes clear which test measures need to be part of the test strategy. Most likely test measures are used that are described in this book. Execution of testing with regard to implementation is where testing cloud services is most similar to a traditional testing process. Chapter 5, Test Measures, contains several practical peculiarities that are of use to the test manager.

A step-by-step plan during implementation encompasses the following activities:

1. Executing the risk analysis
2. Setting up the test strategy
3. Executing the test measures
4. Issuing advice

The risk analysis needs to specifically focus on the cloud and the number of nonfunctional aspects that require attention from the test team. This means that in executing the test measures, experts are needed. At the completion of testing, advice is issued supporting the decision of whether or not to take the service into production. Execution of a proof of concept (see definition in the glossary) can be part of the implementation stage. The objective is to gain further information on the best way to execute implementation. See Chapter 5 for a description of the test measures.

3.2.3   Production

The tasks of the test manager do not stop after a successful implementation. The test manager needs to keep a grasp on changes that occur with the customer, with the supplier, and in the network that connects them.

The following set of tasks is to be performed in production:

- Ensure continuity as changes are implemented
- Monitor the quality of the service
- Review the original selection criteria

The test manager contributes to ensuring the continuity of the business processes by setting up and executing a continuous E2E regression test. The quality guarantees from the supplier need to be verified. The verification can be done by means of monitoring. Eventually, changes can occur that require the review and amendment of the selection criteria and confirmation that the service being provided is still the most appropriate one available for the organization. Section 5.9 describes these activities in detail.

3.3   Testing with the help of the cloud

Meanwhile many testing services are offered under the name Testing as a Service (TaaS). In this book, TaaS is seen as a form of test outsourcing: having test activities executed for a certain amount of money in certain conditions, in this case in the cloud. The boundary between TaaS and using the cloud for a test activity cannot be pinpointed exactly and in fact is not very important. With the use of the Test Outsourcing Governance Approach (TOGA®), we will describe how test outsourcing can best be handled. In a number of examples, we will also describe the use of the cloud for testing purposes.

3.3.1 Test outsourcing to the cloud with TOGA

TaaS is fully in development; there are even forums and testing marketplaces where customers can request test services. The customer of the test service provides an application (a web-based application that can be accessed over the Internet is easiest), and it is subsequently tested. The testing of a webshop can be executed by a TaaS supplier without too many specific requirements because the functional and nonfunctional requirements are quite generic. Testing a custom application for an internal work process, however, requires a large set of specifications to be sent to the supplier in addition to the test object.

When testing activities are outsourced over the Internet, a lot needs to be done to make sure it goes well. Outsourcing testing is special; testing is "the final gateway to go live." A thorough assessment is needed of the quality of the information system and of the risks that potentially remain when going live.

Four (test) outsourcing stages are identified by TOGA:

- Initiation
- Setup
- Transition
- Operation

Initiation

Why is it of interest to outsource testing to the cloud? What objective is served by awarding a test assignment to a TaaS supplier? There are a number of possibilities:

- **Increase performance**: Testing can be done better by others (cheaper, with better quality, faster).
- **Focus on core activities**: Personnel and resources need to target the organization's core activities, and testing isn't one of them.
- **Utilize new opportunities**: In the cloud, new opportunities arise, such as crowdsourced testing (see section 3.3.2) and other forms of collaborative testing.

Which test activities can go into the cloud? There are several options, such as the system test of a website over the Internet, a performance test, or a multi-platform test. There are three steps in the approach to outsourcing testing to the cloud:

1. List options
2. Evaluate which objective is served
3. Determine the impact on the organization

The end responsibility (and with that, control and acceptance) for properly functioning information systems can never be outsourced completely. Take, for instance, acceptance testing: functional acceptance testing can easily be outsourced; the execution of a user acceptance test cannot because it needs to be executed by users.

There are many forms of test outsourcing, of which TaaS is a new variation. Offering a test assignment to the cloud is similar to offshoring (outsourcing to a location far away with a low cost structure). Communication is most likely only in English, is indirect (questions and answers), and can be misinterpreted in many different ways (different culture, different native language, different context). Expectation management is a big challenge. Simple, well-defined test assignments have the biggest chance of being outsourced successfully using TaaS. However, there are test suppliers that offer a large assortment of TaaS products, in which traditional test services with regard to test outsourcing has had a new coat of paint.

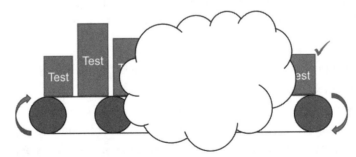

Which test activities can go into the cloud?

Setup

Selecting a testing service is the same as is described in section 5.1. The focus here is, of course, on testing.

Selection criteria are as follows:

- Which organization is behind the service (reliability, stability)?
- What is its reputation; are there references available?
- Is testing a core activity; are standards applied?
- What is the organization's test experience (for instance, built up in the pre-cloud era)?
- How extensive is their domain knowledge?

The customer might consider an audit to assess the quality(ies) of the supplier. The testing world has various suitable methods for this, such TMMi and TPI (NEXT). There are companies that offer these audit services, even as TaaS.

The contract in test outsourcing is of great importance. One buys test coverage, but how can this be measured?

Normally, contracts are detailed with regard to the depth of testing, how tests will be conducted, and how the results will be reported; in short, contracts consist of a set of statements that fit well in the structure of a (generic) master test plan. With the use of test services as they are offered, it can be quite difficult to determine how a supplier achieves test coverage.

Clarity needs to be reached on the following points when test activities are outsourced (not an exhaustive list):

- Which standards are used?
- How are test cases created?
- How are product risks translated to tests?
- What is the estimation method?
- To what extent is the test environment like the production environment?
- How are progress and quality (metrics) reported?
- How will the supplier communicate with the clients?
- What test basis is needed?
- How is the test basis determined for quality?
- How is success measured?
- How is knowledge transferred (domain, system, project)?
- How are legal and financial matters handled (secrecy, rates)?

Transition

With the transition to test outsourcing, a transfer of knowledge, documentation, material, and possibly even personnel happens. The supplier needs to know certain information, such as the URL where the test object can be found, the environment requirements, or the different platforms on which an information system needs to be tested. The test object also needs to be transferred to the test supplier. Transfer of personnel is not very likely with TaaS.

Operation

There are various reasons to keep an eye on testing in the cloud:

- Warranties on quality of testing
- Timely view on outcomes (especially when it is not going correctly and adjustments are needed)
- Information for acceptance (building confidence)

Before testing in the cloud commences, the customer must agree with the supplier about the delivery of information on testing and on test progress.

To enable the customer to monitor the testing in the cloud, initially the customer inspects the test documentation from the supplier. This enables a view to be taken on the quality of the testing. Relevant test documents are test plans, test specifications, and test reports. Then, insight to the test progress and the quality of the test object in the cloud is important. With this, the customer gains a timely view of the expected outcome of the test process. Visibility of metrics is a precondition for a successful check of the outsourced test activities. The following list includes some standard (minimum) metrics for this:

- Trends in the number of unsolved issues
- Trends in the number of found issues per day or per week
- Trends in the number of successful and unsuccessful test cases executed (against the total number of test cases)

3.3.2   Crowdsourced testing

A special form of TaaS is the testing of a test object by "the masses" (crowd). This, in fact, has been done for years: popular software (such as operating systems and games) is offered for free in beta quality so that people can work with it. When users register issues, they are sometimes rewarded with money or full versions of the software. In this way, test coverage that could never be achieved by an in-house testing department is realized. There are also suppliers that organize crowdsourcing for customers. How does one gain a comprehensive view of the test coverage in crowd testing? Metrics for each issue (number and location in the software) are important. Fault seeding can be considered—the deliberate "sowing" of a number of bugs in the software. As soon as all the bugs are found (harvested), the tester can have sufficient confidence in test coverage.

3.3.3   Test environments in the cloud

What can be done for the production environment is also an option for the test environments: creating the environments in the cloud (IaaS). This is an option for test environments that are not needed year-round. Thanks to pay per use, the costs of test environments can be lowered and the temporary setup of extra test environments is a technically and financially feasible option. Following are some examples of the possibilities that test environments in the cloud offer.

Making a snapshot of the virtual environment

IaaS consists of virtual environments. The beauty of it is that when an issue arises, a snapshot of a complete virtual environment can be stored. The environment is released after that, thus reducing the client's expenditure and allowing testing to continue. Later, the same environment can be rolled out again. Using the environment snapshot, issues can be repeated and analyzed. The configuration during the incident is known.

Making a representative test environment

In addition to lower costs, functional advantages can be gained from test environments in the cloud. When the information system to be tested runs on a cloud infrastructure, one can create a fully identical test environment by using the same IaaS configuration that was used for the production environment. Nothing needs to be created in duplicate, as would have to be done in-house.

Executing a portability test for mobile resources

The cloud also offers the opportunity for testing software or sites in all possible hardware and software configurations. With the rise of "the New World of Work" and "Bring Your Own Device (BYOD)," the number of different supported devices has exploded. It is not feasible for an organization to buy and manage a current, representative set of devices for testing purposes. When environments are shared in the cloud with other customers, a test facility becomes available with a wide coverage of different platforms, operating systems, browsers, and so on.

> *Example. There are companies that offer an environment in the cloud in which practically all mobile devices can be tested. The investment that a company needs to make to manage such a set cannot be justified, but in this cloud solution, the costs are divided between the customers. Customers can send their test cases to the cloud and indicate on which devices they need tests to be executed. Cameras that are aimed at the devices can be checked to confirm that the test cases are actually executed.*

3.3.4 Generating load

Heavy load

To test performance, it is necessary to generate load. Performance test tools put high demands on the computers they run on, especially when a heavy load and/or an extremely high number of virtual users need to be set up. Using an infrastructure from the cloud to build a temporary environment to run performance test tools is a possible option.

Worldwide load

For the realistic testing of an Internet application with regard to worldwide use, the load needs to be generated from different locations. There are test services that execute (coordinated) performance tests from different data centers spread all over the world.

4 From Risk to Test

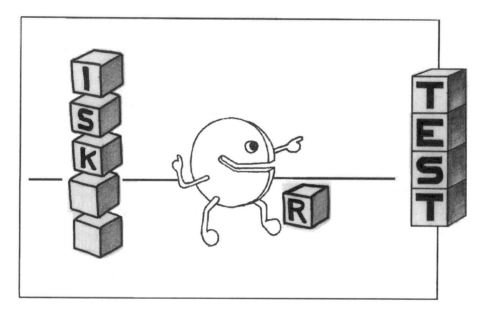

From the essential characteristics of cloud computing, a number of risks can be immediately determined. For example, broad network access means that most services are offered over the Internet, which introduces security risks. A further example is that resource pooling means that devices are shared with other customers, so response times of the service are affected by these other customers. This introduces a performance risk.

The chosen implementation model also affects the risks, especially the severity of the risks. The security risk in the private cloud is less than in the public cloud where other customers have access to the same service.

To determine which test measures are needed, all risks need to be mapped. For testing of services, this is no different from traditional test processes. By conducting a product risk analysis on the service, the areas that are important enough to test, and how stringent testing needs to be can be determined. Chapter 3 described (product) risk analysis.

This chapter contains a collection of cloud-related risks. We indicate which test measures can be taken to cover every risk. Risks and measures are based on practice and are meant as a source of inspiration; they are not exhaustive, but do provide guidance. This is the basis of *Testing Cloud Services* and, as such, the starting point of the test approach.

The risks are grouped to help determine which specialists are needed and to ensure that the list of risks is complete and the risks are sufficiently detailed. People with the right expertise are needed for each topic covered in the risk analysis. It is important that the relevant risks are recognized and that test measures are assigned.

The following risk groups are identified and elaborated on in this chapter:

- Performance
- Security
- Availability and continuity
- Functionality
- Maintainability
- Legislation and regulations
- Suppliers and outsourcing

The relationships between risks and test measures are not one to one but vary. For one risk, more than one measure can be deployed, or one measure can cover different risks (see Figure 4–1).

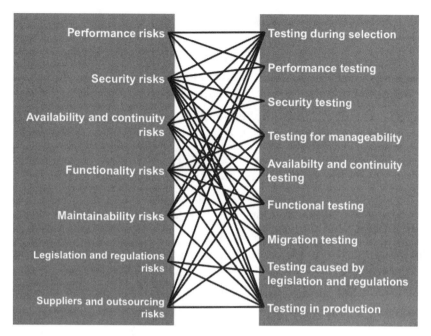

Figure 4–1   *Relationship between risks and test measures*

4.1   Performance risks

Risks concerning performance have been an important focus for a long time. With cloud computing, more communication is done over the Internet, which makes performance risks more significant. Think about the performance of a travel-booking website that is hosted in the cloud. When visitors to the website have to wait too long, they will quit and book their travel with another agency. The first travel agency suffers loss of revenue. In this example, it is easy to get an understanding of the importance of the Internet connection: it is used to reach the (systems of the) travel company. When different systems are used with the help of cloud computing, it is not clear right away that Internet connections are involved. The interfaces with external services and the use of the Internet introduce performance risks in all business processes that use these services. The risk of losing one customer is compounded by the risk that employees of the company are unable to book any travel and can't help any customers.

An important argument in choosing cloud computing is scalability of the service. When more capacity is needed (because performance or accessibility drops), it often can be obtained from the cloud quickly and automatically. Subsequently, it can be scaled down when the need decreases. This facility is called elasticity, and it calls for a new, cloud-specific test: does scaling capacity up and down work efficiently and effectively in practice?

The supplier's model for generating turnover is based on deploying IT resources as efficiently as possible: as many customers as possible using the least amount of resources will, of course, generate the most profit. The supplier will count on the fact that the peak load of the different customers will not coincide—whether this can be justified or not. This means that the service can be overbooked, especially when the service is more successful than anticipated, with the result that the performance of the service decreases. That is because the customers together stress the service more severely than was anticipated. This risk is larger for public and community clouds because the uncertainty of third-party use is largest. In the private cloud, IT resources are not shared with unknown customers and only one customer's services run on it, which lowers the risk in this situation.

An important step in selecting a service is to determine how the user experiences the performance of the service. Messages over the Internet require a certain amount of time to get from A to B. For users, this so-called "latency" can result in a noticeable (annoying) delay. When large amounts of information have to be exchanged, limited capacity in the connection between customer and supplier produces a risk. The user experience is a subjective experience at first, but when business-critical processes cannot be executed fast enough, it can lead to additional resource (people) costs or loss of revenue.

Table 4–1 contains an overview of performance-related risks.

Table 4–1 *Performance risks*

Risk	Test measure (section number/s)
Response times result in problems: – Too high – Increase too much at expected peaks – Increase too much at unexpected peaks	5.2
Processing capacity (throughput) is insufficient.	5.2.1
Upload/download speed (bandwidth) is insufficient: – On supplier side – On customer side	5.1.3, 5.2.1 5.2
Other customers affect performance.	5.1.3, 5.2.1, 5.2.4
Performance is insufficient due to overbooking at supplier side.	5.2.1, 5.9.2
Performance is not sufficient on all types of devices.	5.2, 5.9.2
Customer experiences performance is insufficient.	5.1.3, 5.2.1
Scaling does not suffice: – Scaling up manually does not work. – Scaling down manually does not work. – Manual scaling causes disruptions. – Scaling up automatically does not work. – Scaling down automatically does not work. – Automatic scaling causes disruptions. – Insufficient growth potential.	5.1.3, 5.2.4
Performance varies due to Internet connection.	5.2, 5.9.1, 5.9.2
Performance decreases due to changes by supplier.	5.2, 5.9.1, 5.9.2
Performance deteriorates over time.	5.2.3, 5.9.1, 5.9.2
User demands change over time.	5.9.3

Risk	Test measure (section number/s)
Pay per use not accurate enough: – Paid too much – Too little transparency	5.2.4, 5.9.2 5.1.3
Latency (delay) is too high: – Insufficient performance – Technical issues in the service – Technical issues in the interfaces – Technical issues in interfacing systems	5.2, 5.9.2
Performance is not sufficient throughout the world.	5.2.7
User experiences quality of video or audio as low.	5.2
User requirements for performance are not clear.	5.1.2, 5.2.5
Executing performance tests is not possible.	5.1.3, 5.4.4
Performance tests are not representative.	5.2.11, 5.4.4

4.2   Security risks

What goes for performance also goes for security: it is a topic that regularly appears on the agenda of the test manager. Going to the cloud means that security risks have to be addressed explicitly. Security incidents can result in immediate corporate damage and laws can be violated. There is a lot of regulation on information security and privacy. Risks resulting from legislation and regulations are included in a separate risk group (see section 4.6).

It is remarkable that security in the cloud, most of the time, is better than outside the cloud. For example, a company might have an email server in a cupboard, where anyone can access it. Service suppliers need to address and explicitly organize physical security.

Sharing IT resources with other customers produces security issues. A security error can allow a customer to see and possibly amend data that is not their own. In all implementation models of cloud computing, there is the danger that an employee who has no authorization obtains access to sensitive data. It is necessary to map these risks and cover them if possible.

Purchasing a service implies that, behind the scenes, the IT resources comply to all modern requirements for security against hackers and other criminal activities (cybercrime). This is a crucial part of the service selection process. Vulnerability of the connection between the customer and the supplier can produce a weak link. This has to be taken into account when the risks are inventoried. In short, are storage and transport of data safe enough?

A positive feature of the cloud is the unlocking of the Internet, through which services can be obtained everywhere and on all kinds of platforms. This is consistent with the BYOD trend: employees using their own devices for their work. This results in a new vulnerability. How safe is the device and how safely does the user use it? BYOD is enforced by the New World of Work. People more often work from different locations, most outside the office (and the office network) and use their own devices. Who does not have their email on their smartphone? The company of the employee has little control over all of these aspects and it results in security risks. The question is to what extent policy for information security covers these risks.

Complying with legislation and regulations is discussed in section 4.6. However, there also is legislation that directly brings with it a risk to the security of data. An example of this is the US Patriot Act, which, under certain conditions, raises the possibility that company data that is stored within the jurisdiction of the United States will be accessed.

Table 4–2 contains an overview of security-related risks.

Table 4–2 Security risks

Risk	Test measure (section number/s)
Buildings insufficiently protected against break-in	5.1.3, 5.3.2
Authentication is insufficient: – Other customers (possibly competitors) gain access. – Unauthorized people gain access. – Authorized people cannot gain access. – Customer gains access to other customers' data.	5.1.3, 5.3.5
Authorization is insufficient: – Too few roles and functions can be defined on the customer side. – Too few functions are assigned different access rights. – Administrators on the supplier's side are not sufficiently restricted from accessing client data.	5.1.3, 5.3.6, 5.6.13, 5.9.2
There are too many people that can access everything (on the supplier side).	5.1.3, 5.2.9
Data is accessible through insufficient encryption: – By customer – On network – By supplier	5.1.3, 5.3.4
Service is insufficiently robust against attacks by hackers.	5.3.7, 5.3.10
Data is lost: – Storage device error – Errors in encryption – Loss of encryption key – Scaling (including elasticity) – Procedural errors – Software errors	5.5 5.3.4 5.3.4 5.2.4 5.4.6, 5.4.7 5.6
No access to data because of a business incident on the supplier side.	5.1.3, 5.5.5
Unauthorized people have access to data because of unsafe user behavior.	5.3.3
(Un)authorized access is not traceable.	5.1.3, 5.3.8
Security is not up to date: – On supplier side – On connected systems (customer) – On user devices (customer)	5.4.7, 5.9
It is unknown if user's own devices are safe.	5.3.3
Data is unintentionally not (fully) deleted.	5.6.13, 5.7.6
Disruption of the (virtual) environment by others occurs.	5.9
Third parties obtain access due to summons or investigation (jurisdiction, for example, the US Patriot Act): – Company data – Logging data	5.8

4.3   Availability and continuity risks

When a service is not available at a given moment, it immediately has a disruptive effect on the business processes that use it. Different problems can occur, such as, for example, losing the Internet connection, a device error in the service itself, or no access to company data. The risk analysis will have assessed which disruptions in availability can occur and what negative consequences can be experienced. Depending on the risk, specific test measures are taken for risk mitigation.

Dependency on the Internet is an important risk. What happens when the connection is lost? Does nothing work anymore? Does the company come to a standstill? Is it possible to temporarily work offline, as is the case with writing emails, which are sent automatically when the connection is restored?

Generally in the service provider's terms of delivery or in a service-level agreement (SLA), availability guarantees (or, more often, promises) are stated. Often it is a percentage, but that doesn't mean much. Availability of 99.9 percent means that the service is down a maximum of eight hours and forty-five minutes a year. But if that means that a company cannot operate for one entire day, it can result in considerable disruption. In short, what happens when an incident occurs, how quickly is the service back online, which offline alternatives are available, and do they suffice in practice?

Sharing IT resources, as will occur in the public and community clouds, can also lead to surprises in the field of continuity. When the environment is shared and is the target of a distributed denial of service (DDoS) attack, the service comes to a complete standstill. This will also be a problem for any other customers that use the same environment. It is important to think about this risk at the time of selecting a service.

Are there arrangements for when the service provider goes bankrupt? Is a backup plan available? Does the backup plan work?

Table 4–3 contains an overview of availability-related risks.

Table 4–3 Availability and continuity risks

Risk	Test measure (section number/s)
Connection to the Internet is disrupted: – At the supplier – At the interfacing systems (customer) – At the user devices (customer)	5.5.7
The Internet connection is disrupted at other locations around the world.	5.5.7
The service is partially (not) available.	5.5, 5.9
The offline functionality does not work properly (no synchronization).	5.5.9, 5.6.11
The business process is disrupted by problems with migration: – Missing data after migration – Data changed during migration – Transactions lost during migration	5.7, 5.6.1, 5.9
Data has become unreadable: – Because of hardware failure – Because of loss of encryption key	5.5.6 5.3.4
Data is lost "somewhere."	5.5.3, 5.9.2
Bankruptcy of the service supplier threatens the continuity of business processes.	5.1.3, 5.9
There is no backup plan.	5.5.8
Responsibility for continuity failure is not clear because multiple suppliers are involved.	5.1.3
There are insufficient agreements in place about availability.	5.1.3

4.4   **Functionality risks**

Choosing a SaaS product is a lot like selecting off-the-shelf software: the primary consideration is the features of the software. The risks, therefore, are much like the risks found in selecting and implementing off-the-shelf software. For example, the service is not always exactly according to requirements, so customization will be needed. A service is used to support business processes. Because the service is not, or not fully, meeting the functional requirements, it has an impact on the business processes. A community cloud might involve a lower risk in this case because it is focused on supporting processes in a certain industry.

The service has to be able to work with devices that a customer wants to have supported, such as smartphones, laptops, and desktops. The New World of Work and BYOD ask for proper service compatibility to different platforms, on hardware (PC, iMac, mobile devices) as well as on software (browser versions, operating system versions). For a supplier, it is difficult to ensure that the service works on all combinations of hardware and software. What is the risk of certain platforms not working properly with the service?

A service often has to integrate with other systems. The risk in this is that E2E business processes do not function properly (anymore). This is a possibility when starting to use a service as well as when the supplier deploys newer versions of the service, announced or unannounced. Is the correct E2E functionality still guaranteed in this case?

An important implementation aspect is migration. For the customer, it is important to determine which risks accompany migrating to the service. The exit strategy also has to be considered: moving back out of the cloud or changing to another service (supplier). From a functional point of view, the capability of importing and exporting data in particular has to be assessed.

A specific function of the cloud is the process of requesting, obtaining, and paying for additional service capacity. This function has a direct impact on the business processes. For example, if additional capacity is requested but not granted, the business processes will be disrupted due to capacity shortage.

Table 4–4 contains an overview of functionality-related risks.

Table 4–4 *Functionality risks*

Risk	Test measure (section number/s)
Service and business processes do not align: – Service does not meet all requirements of the business processes. – Using the service results in the need for business process changes. – Service does not work well in E2E business processes. – Service provides insufficient means for configuration.	5.1.3, 5.6.1
Users are not comfortable with the way the service works.	5.1.3, 5.6.3
Quality of the service is inadequate (bugs).	5.6
The manuals are inadequate.	5.4.1, 5.4.2, 5.4.3, 5.6.1, 5.6.3
Service is not according to the supplier's description.	5.4.1, 5.6
Repairing user errors is not possible.	5.1.3, 5.5.4
Functional maintainability of the service is insufficient.	5.4, 5.6
Devices, operating systems, and browsers are not adequately supported.	5.1.3, 5.6.9
Configuration is not done correctly.	5.6.5
Customization: – Is needed but not possible – Does not function properly on supplier side – Does not function properly on customer side – Is not robust when changes are implemented	5.1.3 5.6.6 5.6.7 5.4.8, 5.9.1
Data is not recorded due to insufficient disk quota.	5.2.3
Service implementation: – Has an impact on ongoing business – Causes problems with migrating data to the service	5.7
Service does not match the technical infrastructure of the customer: – The service cannot be properly integrated with other services. – The service cannot be properly integrated with the customer's in-house applications. – Customization is needed for integration.	5.1.3, 5.6.4, 5.6.5, 5.6.6, 5.6.7
Migration problems: – Into or out of the cloud – From one service to another	5.7
Changes are made to the service: – Announced – Unannounced	5.4.7, 5.6.12, 5.9.1

4.5 Maintainability risks

The supplier performs different forms of service maintenance. As a result, the customer has no control over maintenance. How does that work in repairing error situations? Traditionally, this is an important task of the support department. It has to be clear how it is organized and if it works in practice. For administrators, this is a new field of expertise in which not much experience has been built up.

Service suppliers deploy new versions of their services on a regular basis. This is announced, but often also happens without informing the customer beforehand. From a user perspective, when no apparent changes have been made, there is no problem. But when, in fact, something does change, it may require action on the customer side, such as updating work instructions or amending interfaces. When the customer has not been properly informed (yet), it imposes a maintainability risk. Determining the impact from changes to the service is actually, given the often limited information provided by the supplier, a difficult task.

When choosing a service, one does not immediately think of having a test environment because the supplier itself will test the service. However, there is a need for the customer to have a test environment with regard to the service. For example, the customer may need to test changes in the configuration or setup of the service, test customized parts of the service, test interfaces to changed systems, or test the E2E process. The absence of test environments is a risk for maintenance. Fortunately, the cloud also provides endless possibilities for using *on-demand* test environments.

Where does one go to when problems emerge in using the service? Where does a customer report and log issues? The service supplier is not inclined to take up all issues quickly. The risk that can emerge is a back-and-forth of problems and the accompanying issue of blame. This is a well-known phenomenon in outsourcing.

Table 4–5 contains an overview of maintainability-related risks.

Table 4–5 Maintainability risks

Risk	Test measure (section number/s)
Environments are not available for the following purposes: – Testing the service – Testing performance – Testing the E2E business processes	5.2.12, 5.4.4, 5.9
Documentation from supplier is no longer correct after the service is modified.	5.4.1, 5.6.12
Customer documentation is no longer correct after the service is modified.	5.4.2, 5.4.3, 5.6.12
Supplier documentation is insufficient.	5.4.1, 5.6
Business process descriptions are not up to date.	5.4.2
Test documentation from supplier is insufficient.	5.1.3, 5.4.5
It's difficult to incorporate the service in an (automated) test setup.	5.1.3, 5.4.8
There are problems with repairing error situations.	5.1.3, 5.4.6, 5.4.7
IT landscape is not fully under in-house control.	5.1.3, 5.4.4, 5.9
There is insufficient experience with cloud computing.	All sections
Problems with the supplier's issue procedure: – It's not clear. – It's not available. – It does not work properly.	5.1.3, 5.4.6
There is insufficient support from the supplier's help desk.	5.1.3, 5.4.6
There is no change procedure.	5.1.3, 5.4.7, 5.9.1

4.6 Legislation and regulations risks

When using the new opportunities that cloud computing offers, companies need to take into account certain legislation and regulations, such as, for example, local and international privacy legislation for the storage and processing of personal data. Cloud computing is a worldwide market that does not consider national borders, and as a result resides under more than one jurisdiction. Because of this, the user of the service will have to obey different and sometimes even conflicting legislation. Not complying with a law will, of course, result in a risk.

Legislation and regulations can also be risks in and of themselves. There are situations in which company data is securely stored but the government of the country in which the data is stored can still gain access.

Table 4–6 contains an overview of legislation- and regulations-related risks.

Table 4–6 Legislation and regulations risks

Risk	Test measure (section number/s)
Processing and storing data do not comply with some laws: – Laws in home country – Laws in other countries in which the data can reside	5.1.3, 5.8
Countries have conflicting laws.	5.1.3, 5.8
Legislation is unclear.	5.1.3, 5.8
It is not clear where data is stored, which causes uncertainty about legal risks.	5.1.3, 5.8, 5.9
Legal issues arise when the service is down.	5.1.3, 5.8
There is no agreement with the service provider about safe handling of data.	5.1.3, 5.8
Legislation changes.	5.8, 5.9.3
Reliability of a regime in a country is questionable.	5.1.3
Third parties gain access to company data by citation or investigation (jurisdiction).	5.1.3, 5.8

4.7   Suppliers and outsourcing risks

Going to the cloud may be the ultimate form of outsourcing, unfortunately including the accompanying risks. These risks mostly are related to supplier dependency. Standard supplier terms and conditions, potentially supplemented with customized contracts or SLAs, have a crucial role. Subjects that are mentioned in contracts and SLAs are dealt with and covered as risks. On matters that are not covered, there are uncertainties and these represent a risk.

It is important to determine up front what happens to the continuity of the service in the case of a business conflict. Does the customer lose control over the service? What are the consequences for the business processes relying on the service? Which types of business conflicts can occur, and is the contract clear enough to determine the effects on the service's continuity? Do the contracts provide sufficient coverage?

It is possible that the service's continuity is so crucial to a customer that clauses in a contract provide an insufficient basis for trust. In such a case, knowledge about the supplier's development and maintenance process will increase that trust. Test results from the supplier or possibly (other) customers can play an important part.

Table 4–7 contains an overview of supplier- and outsourcing-related risks.

Table 4–7 *Supplier and outsourcing risks*

Risk	Test measure (section number/s)
Bankruptcy of supplier threatens continuity of business process.	5.1.3, 5.5.5
Supplier shuts down the service (for example, in the case of conflict).	5.1.3, 5.5.5
There is ambiguity in the contract about the following: – Continuity – Performance – Security – Defects – End of contract	 5.1.3 5.1.3 5.1.3 5.1.3, 5.4.6 5.1.3, 5.7
Customer is dependent on one supplier (vendor lock-in).	5.1.3
There are multiple suppliers (multivendor) who shirk responsibilities toward each other.	5.1.3
Supplier does not support the correct functioning of the service with test results.	5.4.5
There is no test set available to determine the correct functioning of the service.	5.1.3, 5.4.5
Service ownership is handed over to another party.	5.9.1

5 Test Measures

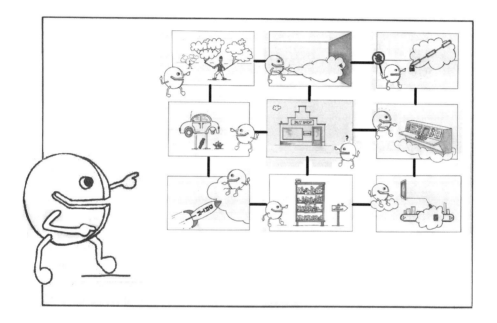

To address the risks in the previous chapter, test measures are needed. In describing the test measures, we pay a lot of attention to test management. In addition, for certain test measures, test specification and test execution is addressed. *Testing Cloud Services* presents a pick and mix of test measures: depending on the risks, one or more measures are picked and mixed.

Where the essential characteristics of cloud computing and the implementation models predominantly affect the risks, the service model affects testing. Testing SaaS is very different from testing PaaS or IaaS. This chapter mostly contains test measures for SaaS; in some places we also address IaaS and PaaS.

The starting point for this chapter is the outcome of the product risk analysis of the service. The result is a list of relevant detailed risks with appointed classification (high/medium/low). For each risk group, this list allows the test manager to determine appropriate test measures. In this chapter, we will describe the following test measures:

- Testing during selection
- Testing performance
- Testing security
- Testing for manageability
- Testing availability/continuity
- Testing functionality
- Testing migrations
- Testing due to legislation and regulations
- Testing in production

5.1 Testing during selection

Generally, during selection, two or more service providers are considered. Too many options cost too much time and energy; too few options limit choice. With new services, it is possible that there is little choice, simply because few suppliers have yet to provide these services.

When a customer is dependent on one supplier, there is what is called a vendor lock-in. When problems arise with the supplier, continuity becomes a risk because there are few or no alternative suppliers to whom the service could be transferred. A vendor lock-in situation puts a customer in an unfavorable situation regarding contract negotiations.

Selecting the most appropriate service and supplier is a time-consuming activity for which budget must be available. Sometimes senior managers or board members of suppliers and customers reach agreement beforehand, and lip service is paid to the selection process.

A pitfall in selection is that the initial objectives may fall by the wayside. This can happen when customers are presented with attractive new services with different options that do not prove to better fit the selection criteria.

Another pitfall is to make concessions to the criteria so that a particular service better fits the requirements.

The selection process is divided into the following steps:

- Include cloud-related aspects.
- Determine completeness and controllability of selection criteria.
- Assess services and suppliers.
- Issue selection advice.

Section 5.1.5 provides a list of possible selection criteria.

5.1.1   Include cloud-related aspects

When the choice is made to go into the cloud, a group of risks are introduced that have to be dealt with. This may lead to certain choices in the selection process, such as choosing a private service rather than a public service, or to choose no cloud solution at all. The risks in Chapter 4 serve as a source of inspiration in the selection process.

5.1.2   Determine completeness and controllability of selection criteria

Selecting a service has significant similarities to selecting software packages: one chooses some kind of standard software package and, consequently, also the supplier that provides the support and updates. There are also differences. With services, the emphasis on "standard" will be even greater than with packages. The more specific the business requirements are, the more difficult it is to find a service to fit. In addition, the supplier's influence over nonfunctional aspects is much larger. For example, with security, performance, and continuity, the customer is largely depending on the service supplier. This is a reason to be extra careful with supplier selection.

Criteria need to be as assessable or testable as possible. If it is not possible to determine whether a service or supplier complies with a certain criterion, this criterion does not contribute to making the right choice. There are different ways to determine whether a criterion is met. These are described in section 5.1.3. Criteria can be improved (become more *smart*: specific, measureable, agreed, realistic, time bound) before the service review by anticipating the review method. Criteria also need to have a weighting factor. A criterion can even be appointed a *knock-out* status, which means that a service or supplier is eliminated if the specific criterion is not met.

Selection criteria for a service

To determine the quality of a service, the required quality needs to be known. For this, functional and non-functional acceptance criteria are incorporated in the selection criteria. In investigating the completeness of the service acceptance criteria, the test manager enters the traditional area of the business analyst: how business requirements are translated into requirements and acceptance criteria for the IT solution (in this case, a cloud solution). An experienced test manager can bridge the world of the organization and IT. An important question is if additional specialty analysis is needed to successfully end the selection process.

The test manager can make an important contribution by performing a review of the criteria that are used for selecting services and suppliers. For the service criteria, this is similar to performing an intake on the test basis for software. For example, completeness and clarity are aspects on which the criteria can be assessed. The test manager can revert to the test basis intake checklists for functional and nonfunctional requirements that are common in testing software.

Selection criteria for a supplier

Choosing a service also means choosing a supplier. When the intended service has to support critical business processes, the customer also has to assess supplier properties during the selection process. Supplier criteria are different from service criteria. To what extent is the supplier of a candidate service sufficiently reliable? Table 5–1 in section 5.1.5 contains questions that can help with this aspect.

The field of cloud computing is still in development. There are suppliers who describe themselves as, for instance, "Cloud Certified Professionals." Though having a certificate does not guarantee quality (a popular theme in testing), it does tell you something about the extent that a party takes cloud computing seriously.

In services, it is not unusual to combine different service models (see Figure 5–1): SaaS with IaaS from another supplier under the hood. For example, Dropbox uses Amazon servers. When Dropbox is chosen, implicitly the choice for Amazon is made. This can backfire (a reason not to choose a service), but it can also work out positively: the verdict depends, in part, on the reputation of the supplier that implicitly is invited along.

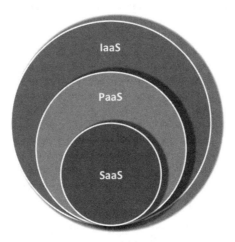

Figure 5-1   *Stacking service models*

A test manager can make a significant contribution by performing an intake on the supplier criteria.

5.1.3   Assess services and suppliers

To reach a reasoned selection decision, information has to be collected about the way candidate services and suppliers comply with the selection criteria and which risks a certain choice implies.

To gain information about a service, the supplier is an important source. The question is whether the customer is limited to documentation on the Internet or whether the supplier can be contacted for more background information, such as information on the way in which quality is guaranteed. When a small customer considers obtaining a simple, standard service from a large supplier, not much "closeness" can be expected between customer and supplier. If the expected amount of work is of sufficient quantity, the supplier will be more inclined to be more transparent.

We next discuss some measures that can be taken during the selection process to learn about the quality and the risks that arise when a particular services and supplier is used. The customer takes the lead, but the role that the supplier can take is also discussed.

Inspect specifications and terms

Generally a supplier will make all sorts of information available on the Internet, such as specifications and terms. From this can be determined whether the service does indeed do what is needed and how load, security, and scalability are arranged. Terms can, for example, contain information about the limitations and rules to which a customer must abide. It may also be possible to determine which types of tests can be performed.

A review of the selection criteria against the service and supplier is done by using the general information the supplier provides. When this information is insufficient, the supplier needs to be contacted. This contact provides the customer with a view of the supplier. How accessible is the supplier and how well do they respond to questions and requests?

Ask for references and certificates

References from and reviews by other customers provide information on how others assess the services or suppliers. Review points that often emerge are recurring problems and outstanding strengths. If the service is part of a community cloud, it is obvious to look for other customers' experiences within the business field.

Standards are available for an increasing number of business fields. When a supplier clearly uses important standards, for example in security, this lowers the risk threshold for cloud computing, simplifies the selection process, and makes different service options more comparable. Reference visits to customers that successfully apply a service can be very convincing.

Specific standards for cloud computing are still in the early stages of development. In an inventory by the NIST in July 2011, three groups of standardization were distinguished:

- Interoperability
  - Self-service IaaS management interface standard. For example, Open Cloud Computing Interface (OCCI) and Cloud Data Management Interface (CDMI).
  - Standard for a functional interface for SaaS (most often through a web browser, and as such not specifically for the cloud).
  - Standard interfaces of SaaS with other systems (not specifically for the cloud).

▪ Portability
  – Standards for cloud workload formats: a way to bring virtual machine images to the cloud. For example, Open Virtualization Format.
  – Data portability. For example, use of Extensible Markup Language (XML) and JavaScript Object Notation (JSON) (not specifically for the cloud).
  – Standardization of workload and data portability still requires a lot of development. An interesting feature of the cloud is "the right to be forgotten." In other words, is data really deleted after a migration?
▪ Security
  – The regular standards in this field.

On the NIST website (www.nist.gov), elaborate tables can be found with standards in the areas of interoperability, portability, and security. It is useful to have an understanding of this when assessing these aspects of a service.

Perform audits and inspections

When the information from documentation and references is insufficiently convincing, an audit or an inspection can be performed to acquire additional information. Using a specialized department or an external party is necessary in this case. Most audits and inspections require supplier cooperation. Here are some examples:

▪ Use a specialist in buildings security to determine whether access control and security camera monitoring for the server location are sufficient.
▪ Use a security audit on the Internet access of the service.
▪ Audit the development and testing process to determine whether the supplier is able to develop qualitatively sound (updates on) services.
▪ Assess test results from the supplier. Insight into the results from tests that the supplier has performed on the service can provide important contributions to an understanding of quality and risks.

Proof of concept

Dynamic testing is also an option—for example, performing a proof of concept (POC). By temporarily using the service, the customer can simulate a situation similar to production in which functional and nonfunctional aspects (such as performance) can be evaluated. Pay per use makes it easier to try a candidate service. Testing of course requires some effort, which has to be included in the cost/benefit evaluation. The selection criteria are the test basis for the POC. A supplier who has a test environment available for performing a POC shows added value.

In the selection phase, the POC is intended to determine to what extent services meet functional and technical requirements. A POC can also be deployed after selection, but the aim will be different: exploring the service and determining the most appropriate way to implement it. A POC evaluation should include the following considerations:

- Determine beforehand when the POC is successful (expected result).
- Define the POC test cases. (Can the service exchange information with system x? Can the service handle the required number of users?)
- Spend sufficient time on preparation (how extensively should the service be tested?).
- Possibly limit the allotted test time (time boxing).
- Consider a second round when the first round leaves questions unanswered.
- Realize that a POC is not intended as a sales instrument for the supplier but is needed to reduce risks.

When an E2E test configuration is available, the service can be temporarily connected. This provides a lot of information about opportunities and bottlenecks that arise with the intended introduction of the service. An E2E test configuration is a good instrument to use to try out and compare different services.

Simulate E2E business processes

When testing a service before final selection or before going live is not an option, the intended new service setup can be simulated. During this simulation, it can be determined whether the service supports the customer's work processes. The processes will be run through entirely or partly on paper, without actually having the service available.

Here are some suggestions for steps to be taken in a process simulation:

- Determine which business processes are included in the simulation.
- Obtain a process description of business processes.
- Create a decomposition of the processes. Which parts are brought into the cloud and which aren't?

- Appoint a business analyst under the supervision of the test manager.
- Make an inventory of all interfaces to the service.
- Test the interfaces between the service and other systems.
- Gain knowledge about the data flow through the E2E business process chain.
- Add adapters to the interfaces (when necessary).
- Run through the processes, using as many live systems as possible.
- Determine whether the service meets the business needs.

An outcome from thorough process simulations may be incidents in existing systems and the business process and a well-documented, refreshed business process.

By replacing a service with simulation software, the customer can try out the integration with the existing system and infrastructure. This is a combination of testing and simulating. There are different kinds of simulation software:

- A stub (catches information from an interfacing system and returns, at minimum, a technical OK signal)
- A driver (provides an interfacing system with previously determined information, from which a process is started)
- A mock (can be used in limited, previously determined situations, responds to information, and provides information on how the mock is addressed)

Check with the supplier whether there is a mock version of the (SaaS) service available.

5.1.4 Issue selection advice

During a selection process, multiple (but not many) services and suppliers are evaluated. It is determined whether or not each selection criterion is met.

Every criterion that is not clearly met represents a risk. A test manager can produce a selection report, comparable to a test report, which summarizes these risks. Not all risks are directly related to IT, such as costs and legal risks. For these risks, input from others is required.

Though a test manager is not the one making the decision for selecting a service, their advice is expected. In the selection advice, the following questions are addressed:

- To what extent are business processes supported? Which services are better, and which ones are less so?
- What are the risks with implementing the intended cloud solution? For example, is private a better option than public to limit security risks, or is IaaS a better solution than SaaS because the in-house software is functioning well but does not have to be running in the in-house data center?
- What are the risks in choosing a particular service?
- How much customization is needed to implement this particular service and which risks occur as a result?
- What are the risks in choosing a particular supplier?

5.1.5 Checklist selection criteria

Table 5–1 contains a checklist of high-level selection criteria, which will need to be modified for your own particular set of circumstances (such as specific test cases to determine the alignment with the business processes).

Table 5–1 Selection criteria

CRITERION	Value/ Range	Weighting factor	Yes/No and Comments
Functional			
Do the service and the specific business processes align?			
Does the service fit well in the E2E business processes?			
Is the service sufficiently adaptable to specific requirements?			
Are many configurations needed?			
Is customization possible?			
Is (a lot of) additional customized software needed?			
Are the required platforms supported?			
Are the New World of Work and BYOD sufficiently supported?			
Is it possible to interface/integrate the service with the other systems?			
Are sufficient manuals and/or courses available?			

CRITERION	Value/ Range	Weighting factor	Yes/No and Comments
Implementation			
Is the impact on current activities acceptable?			
Is a feasible route for migration to the service available?			
Support			
Are changes in the service announced beforehand?			
Are sufficient test facilities available around the service (test environment, test tools, testware, access to infrastructure, etc.)?			
Are there sufficient support facilities?			
Is it clear how incidents can be reported?			
Are incidents resolved fast enough?			
Performance			
Are response times quick enough?			
Is the number of possible simultaneous users high enough?			
Is bandwidth sufficient?			
Is sufficient potential for growth available?			
Is the actual use charged correctly?			
Security			
Are adequate authorization and authentication in place?			
Is the physical security of the service locations sufficient?			
Is the access for maintenance of the service sufficiently secure?			
Is security between customers sufficient?			
Are data changes traceable?			
Is data storage for the service reliable?			
Is deleting data in the service reliable?			
Is security of the connection to the service sufficient?			

CRITERION	Value/ Range	Weighting factor	Yes/No and Comments
Are security options for the customer sufficient?			
Does the supplier have security certificates (for example, SAS 70 type II)?			
Availability			
Is the level of availability for the service sufficient?			
Are backup/failover/disaster recovery provisions sufficient?			
Legislation and regulations			
Does the data location comply with all legal requirements?			
Does the data processing comply with all legal requirements?			
Do any contract terms or conditions conflict with the duties of the customer?			
Supplier			
Is it clear what happens when the contract ends or in case of bankruptcy or conflict?			
Is a good help desk available?			
Does the supplier have experience in the following areas: – Offering this particular service? – Offering services in general? – Developing services? – The customer's field? – Developing, testing and supporting services?			
Do the methods used by the supplier align with those of the customer (if relevant)?			
Is quality assurance performed?			
Is the supplier ahead in its field?			
Is the size of the supplier in accordance with the expectations of the customer?			
Does the supplier have a good reputation (are there references)?			
Is providing services the core business of the supplier?			

CRITERION	Value/ Range	Weighting factor	Yes/No and Comments
Does the supplier have the capability for future expansion?			
Do the supplier and the customer speak the same language?			
Is transparency and flexibility of the supplier sufficient?			

5.2 Testing performance

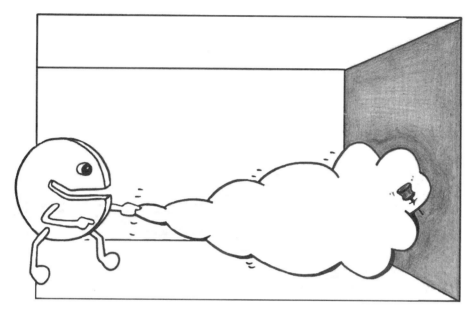

This section is about applying known performance test techniques in the cloud context. In addition, we'll describe an approach to new performance test techniques, such as testing elasticity. However, not all traditional performance tests are run. For example, executing a stress test is in most cases not possible because it jeopardizes the stability of the service for the other customers.

User experience of response times and the system load are key in testing performance. Depending on the identified risks, this leads to a limited or thorough review of different circumstances in which certain performance is desired (during the day, working hours, affects of other users, etc.). Also to be considered is the performance in the case of an (unexpected) increase in user numbers, peaks in load, and prolonged periods of high load.

To determine whether a service meets the performance requirements and expectations, acceptance criteria are needed. What are requirements regarding response times and at which loads do these requirements have to be met? When "going into the cloud," one has to realize that with services it can be difficult to achieve the same response times one is accustomed to.

Introducing more communication steps and the fact that services are not specifically made for the customer are probable factors in slower response times. If it is needed to determine the response times as a result of going into the cloud, the performance on the current infrastructure has first to be measured. The resulting outcome is used as a reference (baseline) with which to compare the cloud performance (see Figure 5–2).

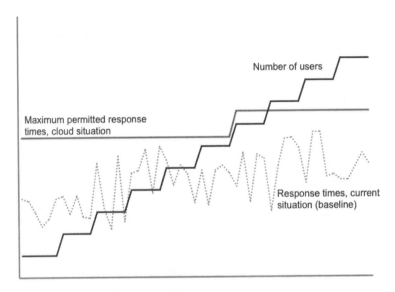

Figure 5–2   *Current situation as a baseline*

With SaaS the center of gravity for performance lies fully with the service provider: they are responsible for the performance that is experienced by the end users (not including equipment and Internet connection speed). With PaaS and IaaS this is more complex because the application and software environments are partially or fully the responsibility of the customer. The performance as experienced by the end user is dependent on the efficiency of the application software (customer), the speed/efficiency of the software platform (customer and/or supplier), and the speed of the infrastructure (supplier). Most performance tests are applicable to all service models. If necessary, the effect the service model has on the preparation and execution of performance tests should be discussed.

The following subsections provide overviews of the different kinds of performance tests and include practical examples for applying these tests to services. In addition, the various aspects of testing performance, such as creating performance test cases, the use of tools, and test setups, will be addressed.

5.2.1   Load test

A load test is a simple test: the tester performs actions on the service as a user would and determines whether the service reacts with sufficient speed and whether errors do or do not occur. This causes a load on the service. The choice of test actions and the applied load depends on the objective of the test. Possible objectives are to determine performance of the service in the following situations:

- Average load (such as the number of users)
- Peak load
- Many users logging on simultaneously
- Many highly active users
- Load during working hours (or other relevant times)
- Steadily increasing load (user organization is growing)
- Steadily increasing number of customers for the service
- Increased load on the Internet
- Suddenly increasing load
- Heavy usage actions (uploading or downloading large files)
- Frequently occurring actions
- Business critical actions

A complicating factor for a service in the cloud is customers not knowing about each other's load on the service. The load on the service by another customer can lead to different metrics from the same test at different times. For this we suggest two things. First, try to obtain information from the supplier about the load statistics of other customers. Second, execute real-time tests. So, if the load test is based on a peak at 8:30 in the morning, actually execute the test around that time. Unfortunately, it will be no guarantee that it also goes well on any other day.

5.2.2   Stress test

A stress test determines the behavior of a service beyond the peak load. This shows what happens to the service when the service load increases more quickly than anticipated or when a sudden, unexpected peak occurs. Traditionally, the test is conducted by increasing the load until the moment something happens. This can be an extreme rise in response times or when a notification emerges, but a stress test can also lead to absolute failure. In the cloud, other parties can be impacted by doing this, so during the stress test the tester needs to stay within the service's terms of use. A service provider, of course, can have fun with this, as long as there are no customers connected to the service that is being tested.

One variation of stress testing that is executable by and useful for a customer is testing the behavior of the system at the edge of the guaranteed load. At or beyond the threshold, will a sensible notification appear, or will performance plummet? Will the situation recover after the load moves back below the guaranteed level? In this case, a boundary value analysis of the guaranteed load is performed. In testing elasticity, this aspect is addressed.

5.2.3   Endurance test or volume test

There are different causes of performance decreasing. Often it results from memory overflow (log files, memory leaks), files becoming fragmented, or the simple fact that finding specific data within an expanding data set is becoming increasingly difficult. After a certain volume is processed, performance drops or the service stops completely. Because real-time execution takes too long, in a volume or endurance test as much volume as possible is input in a short amount of time to get results more quickly. This approach, however, brings risks. Just as with a stress test, a customer can easily move beyond the officially permitted load. Consider also the boundaries that are not explicitly stated but are covered by the term *fair use policy*. A service supplier, of course, is not bound by this: it is even wise to test the service's robustness in this situation.

Performance degradation in production can be an indication of a memory problem, but there are also many other causes (such as an increasing load). Support departments often use memory monitoring tools that show flooding of memory immediately. The customer is able to perform this monitoring themselves with IaaS because a (virtual) environment in which monitoring tools can be installed is provided. This does not provide metrics about the infrastructure but about the software installed by the customer. With SaaS, full responsibility for this lies with the supplier.

5.2.4 Testing elasticity and manual scalability

Testing elasticity is a new aspect of performance testing. The objectives of the test are to determine whether the performance of the service meets the requirements across the entire load spectrum and whether the appointed service capacity scales with the service load. The pay-per-use model is often linked to the elastic aspect of the service. The administrative (financial) handling can become part of testing elasticity.

The approach to this test comprises executing a load test with the load increasing beyond the scaling boundary (scaling up) and then the load decreasing below the scaling boundary (scaling down). Manual actions may need to be performed as part of the test procedure in a process cycle test. Behavior on possible boundaries of packages also needs to be addressed (see section 5.2.10).

The following possible errors can emerge in testing elasticity:

- (Automatic) scaling up does not perform as required.
- (Automatic) scaling down does not perform as required.
- During scaling functional problems emerge.
- Information about use-based costs is not adequate.

5.2.5 Setting up test cases

Performance test cases are based on load profiles. The test load is modeled on requirements such as average, maximum, stress, peak, low. Acceptance criteria, of course, form the test basis, but they are not enough to set up the test cases. Performance test cases are derived from operational profiles. The load is best generated based on actual or expected use of the service. In this way, the tests are as close to real life as possible and test results are sufficiently representative.

Generally, it will not be possible to test the performance of all service functionality. Here, carefully thought-through choices have to be made based on the risk analysis (the operational profiles will provide important input here as well). Load profiles describe the expected numbers of users, preferably accompanied by the time slots in which these users are active. The actions that the users perform will also need to be described. Keep in mind periodical (batch) processes such as invoicing. These processes result in extra (peak) loads at certain times. When more applications run in the same location, this also has to be taken into account. Applications with coinciding peak loads have an impact on performance. In the public cloud, the load from other sources (customers) will be an unknown factor. Based on these profiles, specific test cases are executed, showing if, during certain time slots, the service performs according to expectations.

Setting up operational profiles

When services in the cloud are used, a solution is chosen that is developed by a supplier. Therefore, complete functional descriptions of the service are often not available, and it is likely that the full functionality of the service is not used. To be able to test how the service fits within the current business processes, operational profiles can be used. Operational profiles are descriptions of how a system is or will be used in practice (in production). An operational profile consists of a set of operations, each of which has a level of likelihood of occurring. The operations in the profile can form the basis for test cases, in particular for performance test cases (load profiles), but also for test cases aimed at the E2E business processes. In the book *Software Reliability Engineering* by John D. Musa (McGraw-Hill, 1999), extensive information on setting up and applying operational profiles can be found. Here we include a summary. This approach is a variation on (or addition to) setting up use cases or process flows (see section 5.6.13).

Musa describes five steps for setting up operational profiles.

Step 1: Identify the initiators of operations

This is quite similar to actors in use cases and deals with different types of users, such as an end user, the system itself, another system, or an administrator. It is about who or what performs the operation.

Example. Time sheets

Initiators
Administrator time sheets application
Project administrator
Project employee
Manager

Step 2: List operations

Which operations are performed by the initiators? Focus on operations that differ significantly from each other. Here are a number of tips:

- Use the business processes as a starting point for listing operations.
- Let the degree of detail be dependent on the related risk: more risk, more detail in operations.
- Operations can be recognized by clear differences in the frequency and likelihood in which they can occur.
- Menus and submenus can be useful as an inspiration for listing operations.

Example. Time sheets

Initiators	Operations
Administrator time sheets application	Arrange screen flow Mark obligatory fields
Project administrator	Add project Close project Add project employee Connect project employee to project Add time sheet codes
Project employee	Fill in time sheet each week Release time sheet each week
Manager	Approve time sheets

Step 3: Review listed operations

Experts (such as functional support) review the list, taking at least the following points into account:

- The operations are sufficiently different from each other.
- All possible operations within the application are in the list.

The number of operations in an operational profile can vary from twenty to several hundred. This of course depends on the size of the system. Enterprise resource planning (ERP) systems are generally very large and cover different business processes. Stating the obvious: create an operational profile for each business process.

Step 4: Determine the frequency of operations

Frequency of operations is the number of times per time unit (for example, per hour) an operation is invoked. The most frequently occurring operations form the basis for the load profiles in the performance tests. When a system similar to the one that needs to be tested is in use, the frequency can be measured using log files and observations. In other cases it needs to be estimated (for example, by studying the user process). Time sheet registration, for example, most often occurs on Friday afternoons between 4:00 and 6:00. The total number of registrations is about the same as the number of project employees. The frequency per hour of registering is, as a result, the number of employees divided by two. Time sheets are approved by a number of project managers (this is less than the number of project employees) on, for example, Monday morning between 8:00 and 12:00. The frequency per hour of the operation approval is the number of project managers divided by four.

In measuring the frequency, it is important to carefully study the results: a maintenance process that runs when the load is light can often be found in the log files, but it probably should not receive a lot of attention in testing because the importance of the operation is relatively low.

Step 5: Determine the likelihood of each operation occurring

Here, the share of each operation in the total number of operations per time unit needs to be evaluated so the relative share of each operation is clear.

The likelihood of an operation forms the basis for the attention an operation receives during test execution. Operations with a low likelihood should not be simply discarded. Arranging screen flows can put a very specific load on the system and will, as such, be very useful to include in the test, even when the available time is limited.

Example. Time sheets

Initiators	Operations	Frequency (number/week)	Likelihood
Administrator time sheets application	Arrange screen flow Mark obligatory fields	0.1 0.1	0.0005 0.0005
Project administrator	Add project Close project Add project employee Connect project employee to project Add time sheet codes	0.4 0.4 3 8 20	0.002 0.002 0.015 0.04 0.1
Project employee	Fill in time sheet each week Release time sheet each week	80 80	0.4 0.4
Manager	Approve time sheets	8	0.04
	Total	200	1

5.2.6 Test cases aimed at specific bottlenecks

In the product risk analysis, risks that require a specific dedicated performance test can be identified. Think, for example, of testing certain vulnerabilities in infrastructure. Here are some examples of these risks:

- Insufficient bandwidth in parts of the infrastructure, resulting in an insufficient maximum amount of data per second to and from the service
- Insufficient throughput, which results in the maximum processing capacity of the service being inadequate
- High latency (delay in data transmission between customer and supplier)

In these cases, the load profiles are not based on operational profiles, but the test actions and load will be designed in such a way that the chance of finding a suspected bottleneck is as high as possible. Designing volume test cases is part of this.

5.2.7   Including cloud aspects in test cases

The world

Given the nature of cloud computing, the service used can be located anywhere in the world. It is possible that several different locations are used in the production environment. In addition, particularly with multinational corporations, the service may be used from different places in the world. The results of the performance test may show differences because of these variations. When an overview of the supplier and customer locations is created, this can be taken into account during the performance test.

When a private cloud is used, the relevant locations can be determined relatively easily; with a public cloud, it is very difficult for a customer to gain a view of where the load will come from in practice and from which part of the world without the help of the supplier. When uncertainty about the load on the service by other users poses a significant risk for a customer, it should be questioned whether a public cloud is a suitable service model for this customer.

Suppliers also see these risks, so they are increasingly offering test facilities in which performance tests can be performed on a service from multiple locations around the world.

Customer's resources

Customers are increasingly using more and different kinds of resources. Not only are PCs and laptops connected to services, smartphones and tablets are used more often. Performance can be affected by the type of resource that is used. For each resource type, it is possible to use different networks. Fiberoptics and Asymmetric Digital Subscriber Line (ADSL) will deliver a better performance than General Packet Radio Service (GPRS) or Enhanced Data GSM Environment (EDGE), for example (see Figure 5–3). All these variations will lead to designing extra test cases. The challenge is then to think of test actions that would bring to light performance bottlenecks.

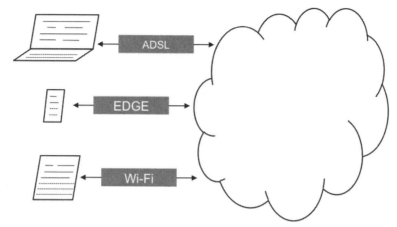

Figure 5–3　　*Bandwidth varies by type of network*

5.2.8　Test cases for the stress test

A stress test is nothing more than a specific load profile to determine the limits of the system. First: determine the boundary value for the maximum load on the service. Suppose this is 100 concurrent users; this leads to test cases with 99, 100, and 101 concurrent users. The expected result is that the performance of the service stays intact for the users, no matter what happens around the boundary value. When no boundary is determined, one can choose a load profile significantly higher than the peak load (taking into account the considerations mentioned in section 5.2.2).

5.2.9　Test cases for endurance/volume test

A load profile of 70 percent of the expected peak load is most often used for the endurance test, stressing the service continuously for a certain amount of time. By doing this, the load during the test remains at a realistic level. The essence in designing the load profile for volume tests is to compact time to shorten the duration of the test: For instance, to test an operation that normally happens once a day, execute it 100 times per minute. It is important when performing this test to keep the contract with the supplier in mind (for example, usage as specified in the SLAs).

5.2.10 Test cases for elasticity

A test approach is described for two situations: one in which scaling up and scaling down happens automatically (true elasticity) and one in which capacity needs to be configured (and released) manually.

During the elasticity test, three test techniques are combined, as shown in Figure 5–4:

▪ Load tests with a load profile to vary loads
▪ Boundary value analysis at the boundaries of scaling up and scaling down
▪ Process cycle test for the administrative process (this will include pay-per-view invoicing)

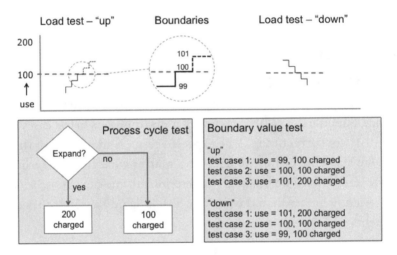

Figure 5–4   *Combining test techniques*

Elasticity (automatic scalability)

The starting point is the assumption that there is a direct connection between capacity use and invoicing. Preferably the load will be increased in such a way that on the supplier side, something actually happens to keep up with the increase and decrease of the load. When that can't be stated with certainty, the load can be increased to twice the current peak load. As a result, an alternative stress test will be executed.

Load profile

Stepwise, the load is increased to the determined maximum; this continues for long enough to be sure that the higher usage will be invoiced. After a predetermined amount of time, the load is decreased again. This also continues for long enough to be sure that the reduced usage will show up in the invoice.

The expected result with regard to the load is that performance complies with the requirements (choose an important operation from the load test as the test case) and that no functional problems occur. The response times are expected to increase and then show a significant decrease after automatic scaling up, as is shown in Figure 5–5.

Boundary values

When the boundary at which capacity will be scaled up is known, boundary value analysis can be performed. The objective is to determine whether there are any disruptions to the service around adjusting capacity.

Process

In principle, one would have to wait for the supplier to send his invoice. As a result, it may take a while until the result of the test is known. When there is an online option to monitor the current invoice in real time, this can be evaluated during the test. Potentially, the supplier's help can be called upon to obtain a copy of the current invoice.

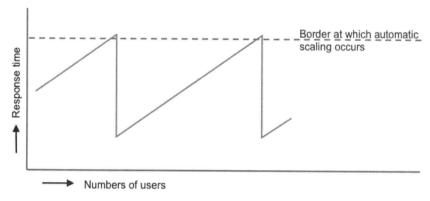

Figure 5–5   *Expected result*

Manual scalability

In this situation, a manual action has to take place to increase or decrease capacity. Here the assumption is made that a certain package with a clearly defined maximum can be upgraded to a larger package or downgraded to a smaller package and that this can be done online.

Load profile

In the first stage, the load is increased stepwise until the maximum is reached. More capacity is not available (most likely). While the load profile is running, the performance and functionality keep meeting the requirements. After more capacity is configured (and allocated), the capacity is increased up to the next maximum. The expectation is that everything keeps working properly. In the second stage, the load is reduced to below the boundary of the previous capacity reached. After the excess capacity is released, the load will be decreased to an average level. The expected result with regard to the load is that the performance meets requirements during the entire process (choose an important operation from the load test as the test case) and that no functional problems occur.

Boundary values

There are specific boundary value cases (the decision has been made for two cases per class).

Normal capacity:

1. Valid boundary value within the maximum of the lower capacity level (performance is within requirements and there are no functional problems).
2. Invalid boundary value, just above the maximum of the lower capacity level (should not be possible, resulting in a warning message; there is no extra capacity configured).

Capacity is increased:

3. Valid boundary value, just above the maximum of the lower capacity level, at the lower boundary of the higher capacity level.

Load goes up and down again:

4. Valid boundary value, at the lower boundary of the higher capacity level (test that it is not possible yet to release capacity).
5. Valid boundary value, just below the lower boundary of the higher capacity level (test that it *is* possible to release capacity).

The excess capacity is released:

6. Performance meets requirements and there are no functional problems.

Process

Check the next control points:

- Configuring extra capacity is possible at any time.
- Releasing excess capacity is not possible when too much is still in use.
- Releasing excess capacity is possible when actual usage allows it.
- The invoice matches the configured capacity.

The exact behavior of services with scaling depends on the way the supplier has configured this process and on the technical implementation. This implementation, which may work in combination with virtualization and load balancers, is still being developed, which is all the more reason to test this thoroughly.

5.2.11 Test setup for a performance test

In a performance test setup (see Figure 5–6), a number of important elements are present:

- **Measurement tool**. Determines response times and is usually a part of a performance test tool that also checks the correct functioning of the service.
- **Load generator**. This can increase the load on the service. It is generally another part of the performance test tool. (Although sometimes performance tests are executed by getting lots of people to do something simultaneously, the majority of performance tests are executed by test tools that simulate users by means of virtual users.)
- **Monitors**. These are able to measure certain aspects of the infrastructure, such as the technical load and the correct generation of error messages. Useful measurements are, for example, use of memory, network load and processor use. The information from monitors (and from log files to check

for error and warning messages) is needed to determine the limiting factors of the bottlenecks that are identified. It is very useful if this information is also collected, analyzed, and reported (preferably in graphs for easier visualization) by the performance test tools.

There are many tools that can test websites and web services, both open source and commercial tools. The advantage of cloud services is that they are generally accessible over the Internet and inherently use a protocol that is suited for the Internet. The majority of tools can handle all mainstream protocols. There are large differences in the extent to which different tools can process information from monitors (see the third bullet point in the preceding list).

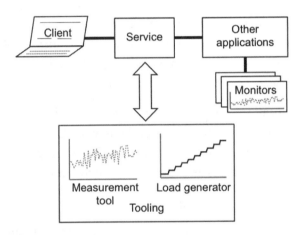

Figure 5–6   *Performance test setup*

5.2.12 Representative test environment

A useful benefit of cloud computing is that service performance tests can be performed in a production-like environment. Tests can be executed on the service even when it is not yet in use. When the service is in use, it can be extended (based on pay per use). However, particularly in the public cloud, no guarantee can be given about the pattern of load on the service by other users. The service provider can affect the load by changing the distribution of users across the infrastructure. This poses a limitation on representativeness over time: today it works correctly, but tomorrow it might be different. This might be a reason to make the performance test part of a continuous system integration test.

Doubling the use of the service by using it for testing purposes seems expensive, but it is a lot cheaper in comparison to purchasing an in-house test environment, which would be needed for non-cloud service applications. Certain organizations are used to take the risk of not testing because a production-like test environment is too expensive. With cloud computing, a lot can be gained in this area though. See sections 3.3 and 5.4 for more information on test environments in the cloud.

5.3   Testing security

To cover security risks, many kinds of measures are possible. The field of security is, just like the cloud, in continuous motion and requires regular research on new and updated measures.

Security is predominantly about *information security*. Different standards exist in this field, such as ISO 27001, which differentiates the following three aspects:

- Confidentiality of the data and the accompanying risk that unauthorized people can view the data
- Integrity of data and the accompanying risk that data is altered or lost unintentionally
- Availability of data and the accompanying risk that data (and services) is not available when it is required

The following three questions correspond to the three aspects of information security:

- Who has access to the data?
- Can the user trust that the data is correct?
- Can the user gain access to the data at all times?

Authorization and authentication are security measures that users, administrators, and other staff notice immediately. Authentication verifies the identity of a person (or system) and their authorization regulates access to data and the actions that are permitted. Authorization and authentication are handled in the application software (the service itself), the operating system, or special security systems (such as identity services). Procedures also determine the success of such security measures (think about managing authorizations and issuing passes).

The quality of the software and hardware is another important aspect of security. Vulnerabilities in software and hardware design are taken advantage of by malicious persons to gain illegal access (exploits). Keeping IT resources up to date and installing the latest security patches are the most important security measures. Not all attacks can be prevented, however; many exploits can be prevented only when programming is done in a secure way.

> *Example. In preventing an SQL injection (example of an exploit), it is important to check all input that can be entered on a page before it is processed. This input needs to be filtered in such a way that unwanted code cannot be executed. By using quotes, the tester can try to alter SQL instructions in the service. The only place to build in this security is in the service's code.*

Encryption on different levels is important and often used as a security measure. Encryption can be applied at the file and protocol levels (Secure Sockets Layer [SSL] and Transport Layer Security [TLS]).

Social engineering (manipulating people to gain access to data), is the most successful way to bypass security measures. That's why people are personally responsible for a number of security measures, such as keeping their login data secure, using an access code on mobile devices, and keeping doors closed.

Next to preventing unauthorized access to data, logging all data transactions and all (whether successful or not) attempts to gain access to data is an important security measure. Not only can digital access to data be logged, but physical access as well. This is possible with security cameras, for example.

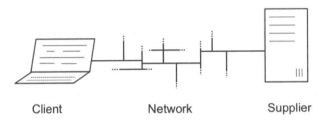

Client   Network   Supplier

Figure 5–7   *Security locations*

Determining the security level of a service starts with inventorying the security measures and is followed by assessing and testing these measures. The entire E2E chain should be evaluated (see Figure 5–7).

The security level that is found during the inventory has to be assessed against the classification (severity) of the security risks that emerge from the risk analysis. In this section we explain which measures a test manager can implement to gain insight in the correct configuration of security measures.

In practice, the test manager will run into several obstacles when determining risks. Not every service supplier, for example, will appreciate a security audit. Understanding the physical security of buildings all around the world is also not an easy feat. The approaches that are described are to provide inspiration, and the future will show what is feasible and what is desirable.

It is important that the service supplier provides information about data security around the service, such as, for example, by handing over audit reports, test results, and security certificates.

5.3.1   Assessing network security

Limited protection can be expected from Internet security. It is impossible to guarantee that the stream of bits (which represents the data) will not be tapped or intercepted. So it is important to make sure that when an unauthorized party gets hold of the data, they can't do anything with it. This can be done by encrypting the data. It is not feasible to provide an up-to-date overview of the most recent and strong forms of encryptions because the field of data encryption is (necessarily) constantly developing.

At a protocol level, encryption can be applied by means of, for example, SSL and TLS. At a network level, different types of encryption exist. For Wi-Fi, Wi-Fi Protected Access II (WPA2) is the most used variant at the moment. Wired

Equivalent Privacy (WEP) is also still being applied, but it is somewhat older and easier to break. The connection between supplier and customer devices can be protected by running it over a virtual private network (VPN).

5.3.2 Inventorying supplier security

First of all, review the location's physical security. How easily can an unauthorized person gain access to the area where servers and system administration consoles are? How is access control organized? Are there security cameras? Once inside, are there opportunities to interfere with the server or take anything away, and if so, what is the effect on the service?

Though a service is offered to customers, the supplier also has access to the service. It is important to know what the supplier's administrators can and are allowed to do. Check how the authorization and authentication process for administrators is organized.

In the private cloud, servers are exclusively set up for one customer. With other forms of the cloud, a server contains data from different customers. How distinct is this split? In what way is one customer prevented from accessing another customer's data? Normally this is done using technology, including authentication and authorization.

Authentication

Authorized persons need to gain access to the service. To do so, they need to go through the authentication procedure. There are different forms of authentication. Some of the most used mechanisms are as follows:

- Login with username and password
- Use of a code, generated by a token system
- Use of an access card
- Biometric data (for example, fingerprints or retina scans)

On the one hand, authentication needs to be as secure as possible. On the other hand, users find it annoying having to repeatedly sign in. There are different mechanisms that support logging on once, such as single sign-on (SSO), network domain, Active Directories, and identity services.

The world of identity management in the cloud is developing fast. There is even a name proposed for it: Identity as a Service (IDaaS). When a trusted institution has determined one's identity, this outcome (identity has been verified) is provided as a service to other parties that do not need to confirm the identity by themselves. DIGID (Dutch government) and OpenID are examples of identity management services. There is an XML-based standard language, Security Assertion Markup Language (SAML), which is used to exchange authentication and authorization information.

As with encryption, the security that authentication offers becomes better when different authentication techniques are combined. With online banking, a valid combination of username and password is always expected. Thereafter, additional authentication differs from bank to bank. Think of filling in a code received via a text message on a linked phone number, or card readers that generate a code based on the bank card.

Authorization

Which role or person can perform which operation, or gain access to which information needs to be verified through authorization processes. This is true for administrators as well as for customers of the service. The degree of trust that the customer has in a supplier is part of it because there are personnel at the supplier who can access everything. Then the limits are reached: who will guard the guardians? (*Quis custodiet ipsos custodes?* The Juvenal dilemma.)

Log files and audit trails

With log files and audit trails, changes to data and attempts to access data are registered. Inspection of the log files shows who has had access. The authorization of those persons can be determined and irregularities can be tracked. With audit trails, changes that systems apply to data also have to be considered. This can also cause unwanted changes in data. For financial institutions, the obligation to make sure that all changes are traceable in an audit trail is increasing.

5.3.3 Inventorying customer security

The software and data that are used in the cloud are accessed from the existing environment. In addition, new devices are used, such as mobile phones and tablets. Security around the resources on the customer side has to be taken into account in the inventory. Ask the following questions:

- Is there authentication and authorization on the customer's network and environment?
- Is there authentication and authorization on mobile devices?
- Are there technical solutions such as firewalls and routers?
- Is an update routine in place for security patches for middleware and operating systems?
- What is the status of the physical security for the building?

On the customer side, the possible unsecure behavior of the user is the main issue. The trend of BYOD makes it an increasing concern. Organizations need to develop policies for the secure use of devices by users as a condition of permitting them to use their own equipment.

Here are some examples of unsecure behavior by users:

- Use of a "remember password" functionality on a computer. If someone is logged on to a computer, anyone who uses that computer can access everything, possibly including the service with the level of access of the person who is logged on to the computer.
- No lock on mobile devices. Leaving devices lying about or losing them allows someone else to gain access to all facilities and possibly to the service—for instance, by way of a mobile application (app).
- Vulnerabilities around passwords (weak or predictable passwords, a note on the back of PCs).
- Susceptibility to social engineering.

5.3.4 Testing encryption

Testing whether or not encryption is activated can be done without extensive specialist knowledge. Most modern test tools are able to test messages with and without encryption, and by comparing them, can determine whether a data stream is encrypted. When storing logon data in a database, check that the password is stored in an encrypted form. Encryption has to be switched on for all resources, including mobile devices and equipment at home.

5.3.5 Testing authentication

Authentication procedures are easily testable with functional test techniques. Think about the syntax test (valid/invalid logon data), process cycle test (authentication issuing procedure), and data cycle test (life cycle of authentication).

Unsafe behavior from people is one aspect that has to be addressed in testing authentication. Users are inclined to choose simple passwords that are easily remembered. For this reason, the software often enforces the use of more complex passwords and changing them on a regular basis. These procedures can be tested with a process cycle test. Ensure that accounts for testing purposes are not entered into the production environment.

In principle, combining authentication mechanisms provides better protection. This may cause unforeseen problems, such as when authentication/authorization mechanisms are not correct for an individual. The test approach will need to include normal and error paths.

Example. Often the authentication for internal and external employees differs. Internally, for instance, an employee can be logged on with domain authentication; externally, authentication with a valid token is necessary. It is expected that an internal logon with a valid token but without sufficient permission in the domain is possible. An example is staff who are allowed access to a specific application, but not to the entire environment. This is a situation that is often skipped in testing and can cause problems in production. It happens that the authentication mechanism authenticates the internal for the domain but does not check any further. In this way the token is not recognized and the internal does not get access to the application for which the token authentication is used.

Authentication methods and their strengths and weaknesses are continuously changing. Staying up to date in this field is the work of specialists. When determining which methods to deploy, you must often seek external expertise. Make use of these specialists to understand methods for testing authentication.

5.3.6   Testing authorization

Functional test techniques are used to test authorization. The test basis is an authorization table (see Table 5–2) in which it is shown what someone with a specific role is and is not allowed to do. The account issuing procedure is tested with a process cycle test in combination with a data cycle test (including revoking authorizations).

The process for checking specific authorization profiles for too many or too few permissions assigned is as follows:

- Have an authorization table at hand; when it doesn't exist, design the table (for instance, with the help of functional administrators).
  - Each group or role has its own record in the table.
  - People can have multiple roles and therefore have different levels of authorization.
  - List possible actions.
  - Checks indicate what is and isn't allowed.
- Test the cells by performing the actions with the specific role and checking whether it is or is not possible (a check indicates that an operation is allowed for this role).
- Test all cells for full coverage.
- Try to gain access to data that only people with the highest authorization are permitted to access (for instance, in the public cloud).
- Try to gain access to data that only people with administrator permissions are permitted to access (for instance, in the public cloud).

Table 5–2 *Example of an authorization table*

User group	Adding users	Deleting users	Manage projects	Filling in time sheets	Approve time sheets	Generate monthly totals
Administration	X	X	X	X	X	X
Project manager	X		X	X	X	X
Standard user				X		X

5.3.7 Testing security robustness against Internet attacks

Security risks are often exposed by hackers through directed attacks. The following types of security attacks on web-based systems occur frequently:

- **Directory traversal**. Read and/or write in directories other than those allowed.
- **XML external entity attack**. Include extra (bad) data in an XML file.
- **SQL injection**. Request and/or change data by manipulating SQL queries.

- **Cross-site scripting (XSS)**. Transfer data to other websites without the user knowing.
- **Session manipulation**. Skip steps or validation in a session.

An example of session manipulation: In a web shop, people can place items in the shopping basket. Next they follow a number of steps to actually order these items. By manipulating the session status, a malicious user skips the payment step, and to the service it still seems like the payment has occurred. Products are sent without being paid for. Systems that administer the session status on the user side (rather than on the server side) are vulnerable at this point.

Testing robustness against attacks requires in-depth knowledge of and experience with test tools. On the Internet, tutorials (hackmes) can be found. These provide basic knowledge on how security can be tested.

5.3.8   Testing log files and audit trails

An important security measure is to track all changes in data and attempts to access data. The testing of these mechanisms is done using functional test techniques, especially for correct flows. For example, execute changes and check whether they are registered in the log files or audit trail.

Make sure that log files are not displayed to the user when error messages appear. Error messages are often the starting point for hackers to gain information about system access.

5.3.9   Testing security patch routines

On the service side as well as the customer side, security systems and other software need to be up to date with the latest security patches. Testing these routines requires checking whether the proper procedures are in place and whether there is evidence that these procedures are followed.

5.3.10 Performing audits

In addition to ISO 27001, there are other standards on which security audits can be based, such as, for example, SAS 70. There are companies that offer audits as a service. There is increasing demand for security reports, as a result of legislation and regulations, for example. To convince potential customers that their data is secure, service providers need to anticipate this demand.

In a public or community cloud, special attention has to be paid to the way in which data from different customers is separated—for example, with separate disks or separate virtual machines. Some audits check physical security alongside software security (for instance, whether there are security cameras and how access is managed).

Specialized test companies can test the robustness of the infrastructure as seen from a customer perspective. So-called white hat hackers are deployed to try to enter the system. These audits provide information on the weaknesses of the system, for which possible solutions are put forward.

5.4   **Testing for manageability**

The essence of manageability is, "How we keep the service and the processes around it in working order." The success of a service depends partly on the systems that exchange information with the service. That is why the E2E processes, of which the service is part, are taken into account during testing. Manageability is closely related to maintainability and is about the ease with which the service can be modified to (be able to) keep it in production. There may be several reasons to update the service (fixing errors, changes in the environment, new requirements).

This book provides a number of guidelines for the test manager in a world that is predominantly controlled by people in administrator roles. As is described in Chapter 3, the distinction between implementation and production is diminishing. In other words, the role of the test manager does not end with a service implemented into production.

Manageability is tested using a checklist. In most cases it is about static forms of testing, but a run-through of administration and maintenance procedures in practice or in a simulation is also a possibility. These simulations are useful for the customer as well as for the supplier. A supplier can test whether the agreed-upon incident response times are met.

Manageability checks for documentation are as follows:

- Is documentation available?
- Is documentation kept up to date?
- Are changed versions sent to the correct stakeholders?

Various specifications are part of manageability and are subject to testing. The specifications discussed in this chapter are important from a testing point of view because they form the test basis and provide important information about test environments.

5.4.1   Specifications on the supplier side

In this section, we look at the specifications that the supplier has to deliver along with the service.

Interface specifications

Services will only run as stand-alone processes in a limited number of circumstances. In most cases, an interface is needed between services and systems that do not run in the cloud. There may also be a need for interfaces to other services, such as connecting an email service to a CRM service. At this point, SOA helps because it uses standard interfaces, often in XML format. Connections to office suites also often occur. The service provider has a duty to have the interface specifications under strict change management. The customers are fully dependent on these specifications for the connections to other systems. From an administrative perspective, the change procedure is subject to scrutiny. For testers, the interface specifications are the basis for tests with regard to the message structures that will be used.

Specifications for customer resources

A special group of systems connected to a service (predominantly SaaS) is formed by the devices by which the service is presented to the users. The service supplier has to be clear about to which specifications these devices have to comply. Different types and versions of browsers and mobile devices need to be kept in mind. Because different configurations are increasingly available, referring to standard specifications such as, for example, HTML5 and other web-related standards is a suitable alternative to specifying many kinds of different devices. With regard to management, it is important to have an up-to-date overview of the device specifications from the supplier. Testing services with multiple devices is discussed in section 5.6.

Platform specifications

A PaaS supplier will install platform software updates on a regular basis—for example, security patches or bug fixes. It is possible that this affects the use of the service by the customer. Having a recent overview of the available platform specifications is subject to a manageability check. IaaS suppliers sometimes offer the option of pre-installed software. For this, the same is true as for PaaS with regard to platform specifications.

Infrastructure specifications

IaaS suppliers base their services on a virtualization layer. This means that software updates also are done there, with possible knock-on effects to the user experience. Changes in the hardware layer can also impact the user. Keeping infrastructure specifications up to date and available is part of a manageability check.

5.4.2   Specifications on the customer side

The customer has responsibility for other specifications.

Infrastructure specifications (IaaS)

The customer needs a blueprint (design) for the infrastructure to be built in IaaS cloud service. The customer is responsible for checking whether the blueprint is available and correct and for choosing the way in which it is maintained.

System specifications

A customer who runs their own software in the cloud will need to have the complete system documentation (the full V-model) available. For the process of creating, testing, and managing this documentation, we refer to prevailing software development and testing processes. In other words, this is not done any differently for the cloud than it is for software running on an in-house environment. The same goes for the software development process of the service suppliers. System specifications are an important part of the manageability checklist.

Architecture documentation

In one way or another, the customer needs to map out how the service is going to be integrated in the (technical) E2E infrastructure. What does the system picture look like? Where are the interfaces? A system picture is needed for every service model (SaaS, PaaS, IaaS) and must be kept up to date. Because of that, it deserves a place in the manageability checklist.

Business process documentation

In addition to the technical aspects of the system picture, there are the business processes that use or are dependent on services and potentially interface with other systems. When there is documentation on business processes available, it needs to be kept up to date (manageability check).

Business requirements

Even when using standard SaaS, business requirements that reflect the business needs will be present. SaaS functions can be linked to the business requirements. In this way, traceability is present and requires maintenance, and so it will be subject to a manageability check.

5.4.3   User documentation

To use a service, an instruction manual is needed. This is true for each service model. When using IaaS, the manual needs to provide relevant information to the person who configures the environment, puts it into production, rolls out software on it, and so on. In the case of PaaS, it is about instructions for rolling out application software and configuring databases or using the development platform. Normally, this is a job for people from the software development department. The user instructions for services target different groups of users. This can be end users but also administrators who configure authorization and process architects who configure the service. In all cases, documentation is needed on how the service needs to be configured, used, and maintained by the customer.

The term *user manual* needs to be interpreted widely. Frequently asked questions (FAQs), lists of known errors, and online courses can be important added sources of information for the user.

In many cases, additional manuals need to be created on the user side—for example, to embed working with the service in the business processes. This is the most likely place to (temporarily) solve deficiencies in the manuals provided by the supplier. The manuals need to be kept up to date; however, in practice this doesn't often receive high priority. When this poses a large risk, escalation to the supplier is an option. Testing manuals is also addressed in section 5.6.

5.4.4   Test environment availability

When moving from traditional testing to testing in the cloud, the necessity for test environments remains. It seems obvious, but it's not always the case. Take, for example, the hosting of a company website (a form of PaaS): frequently there is no or only a very limited test environment available. Through a content management system (CMS), changes to the website are applied directly to production, or only a limited test environment is available; email messages, for example, may not be able to be sent from the website, and as a result, certain functions cannot be tested E2E.

> *Example. A solution for changing the web contents on the production environment is a so-called staging environment. This allows changes in production to be tested before they actually go live.*

In the private cloud, the customer often has access to facilities for test purposes, but in the public cloud, offering of test facilities by the supplier is still in its infancy.

The different service models are discussed next from a development, test, acceptance, and production (DTAP) point of view.

Test environments in IaaS/PaaS

The customer obtains the infrastructure or a platform for production, on which the in-house application software is running. In a regular development process, development, test, and acceptance environments are needed in addition to the production environment. One option is that these do not move to the cloud and they remain under in-house management and fully under the customer's control. As a result, a huge difference emerges between the D-, T-, and A-environments on the one hand and the P-environment on the other. Once the choice to move into the cloud is made, in most cases it is not desirable to keep in-house environments running, and as a result, the D-, T-, and A-environments will also be obtained from the cloud (see Figure 5–8).

The requirements that developers and testers need the environments to meet are translated into extra specifications for IaaS/PaaS. Flexible use of (test) environments can result in an important cost saving and creates the opportunity to have a good copy of the production environment available for test purposes.

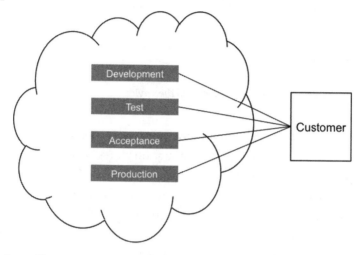

Figure 5–8   *All environments in the cloud*

Test environments of the SaaS user

Because the service is not developed by the customer, no separate D-, T-, and A-environments need to be available for the service. One service environment can, in most cases, be connected to multiple customer environments (see Figure 5–9). For testing the service itself (for instance, trying different setups and options), some suppliers provide a so-called sandbox environment. When such an environment is not available, the service itself will be used as a test environment. This is possible with, for example, test users or by accessing the service with another username or customer name. The activities in this test segment of the SaaS must not interfere with the production activities of the supplier or the customer.

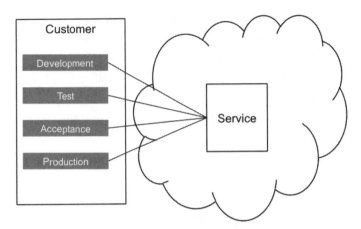

Figure 5–9   *All environments are connected to the service*

Systems connected to SaaS need an environment for testing in combination
with the service, without disrupting production. A test segment of the service
can be used; it is connected to the test environment of the linked systems.
Replacing the service by a mock service (simulator) is also a possibility by
which the linked systems can be tested E2E (see Figure 5–10) independently of
the service's availability. Preferably, a mock service is supplied by the supplier (it
can be an important reason for a customer selecting the particular service).

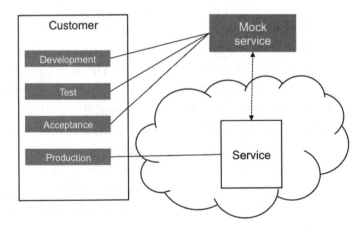

Figure 5–10   *Use of a mock service*

5.4.5   Test documentation

Normally, test documentation is an important part of maintenance documentation. Test documentation is mostly used, for example, to execute regression testing and retesting for patches and infrastructural changes. There are two categories: customer test documentation and supplier test documentation.

Customer test documentation

Keeping test documentation up to date (or having it kept up to date) is the responsibility of the test manager. The distinction between implementation and production (usually the domain of administration) is fading: in production the test manager also has a responsibility toward testing continuity. The manageability checkpoint is to confirm whether maintenance of test documentation is properly organized; for example, acceptance tests, test basis, E2E tests, and issues must be considered.

Supplier test documentation

In principle, this is an internal affair for the supplier. There are, however, reasons why test documentation is shared with customers:

- Publishing test results can gain customer confidence.
- Publishing test procedures enables customers to perform a beta test.
- Making test cases available makes it easier to test interfaces.

Management of in-house test documentation does not deviate from normal software development procedures for the supplier. When a customer uses the supplier's test cases for testing interfaces, these also need to be maintained and are subject to a manageability test.

5.4.6   Incident management procedure

Several scenarios can arise that the incident management procedure has to take into account. The three scenarios in Figure 5–11 are further explained as they relate to the incident management procedure.

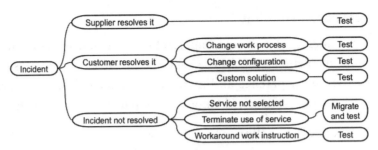

Figure 5–11   *Dealing with incidents*

Supplier resolves the incident

Preferably the supplier has an incident management procedure in which both the supplier and customer agree if and when the incident is resolved. A help desk and/or other forms of support provide the lines of communication between the customer and service supplier. This is similar to a regular incident management procedure, with all its features and its issues, such as discussions on priority, partly resolved incidents, and regression testing. An SLA may contain details about response and resolution times. Service updates can contain resolved incidents. By means of direct communication with the customer, the supplier can indicate in which service version specific incidents are resolved. The update may be rolled out initially onto a test environment, which provides the customer with the option of performing retests and regression tests before going live with the service. In the absence of a test environment, the customer has to retest the resolved incidents on the production environment. Service updates always need to be accompanied by information about changes relevant to customers.

Large customers have an incident management procedure in which all production issues are managed (for cloud and non-cloud systems). In such cases an interface between the supplier incident management system and the customer incident management system is needed. The entire process, from finding an incident on the service to the implementation of the modified service, needs to be managed. All stakeholders (including the service users) need to be informed about the incident life cycle.

When there is no SLA with response and resolution times, the customer is fully dependent on the priorities determined by the supplier. When a high impact issue arises, the customer can try to gain awareness of the problem by way of a help desk or other support procedure. If other customers are also experiencing this problem, the probability of the incident being resolved more quickly increases. An incident always needs to be registered so a supplier can see when the same problem arises for different customers. A supplier will deliver resolved incidents in service updates. Although release notes are published with an overview of the changes, it is unlikely that all registered incidents are specifically listed. The E2E regression test will show that the service has been updated and the incident can be closed. Depending on the severity of the incident, the regression test may need to be updated.

When the customer has outsourced service management, a different scenario arises. In this scenario, the incident management procedure is set up by the third party and will need to be agreed upon in the SLA between the customer and the third party. For production incidents, the third party can sometimes resolve the problem themselves; otherwise, the third party will contact the service supplier.

Example. An IT company supplies IT facilities to a medium-sized company. It is agreed to have the email server in the cloud, provided by a large service supplier. This scenario has advantages and disadvantages with regard to resolving incidents. An advantage is that the company can record incidents with the IT company, who in turn will deal with the service supplier. A further advantage is that the IT company looks after the email services of a number of customers and through this greater usage will get the attention of the service supplier more easily. A disadvantage is that an extra layer is created that could create delays in resolving incidents.

Customer resolves the incident

Certain incidents are resolved by the customer—for instance, by changing the service configurations. An alternative option is not to change the service but to change the business process. With services for more or less standard procedures, this will occur more often. If changing configurations or business processes is not possible, the customer can decide to resolve the incident by customization, such as, for example, resolving incidents on interfaces between the service and other systems by means of an adapter. In all cases, retests and regression tests are executed after the incident is resolved.

The incident will not be resolved

In a number of cases, the incident is not resolved by the supplier nor by the customer. This can occur during selection: because of the incident severity, the customer can decide not to select the service. If a serious (not resolvable) incident occurs in production, the customer may have to decide to change to another service. This requires a migration and all its related test activities. A customer can also decide to use a workaround to bypass the incident. Testing the workaround will in this case encompass checking the work manual in which the workaround is described. In practice, this procedure does not differ much from changing business processes.

5.4.7   Change procedure and version control

While using software and platforms, new requirements arise. This will not be different in the cloud. The customer will need to set up a change procedure. Certain changes can be done by the customers themselves; for instance, by changing the configurations of the service. Other changes will need to be discussed with the supplier. The path from idea to realization (and test) requires management. The purpose of the manageability test is to check whether this is properly organized and includes the updating of manuals.

Continuous integration, which occurs during service use, requires well-organized version control at the supplier side as well as at the customer side. The supplier needs it for making clear to all customers which versions of documentation (technical and functional) are active for which version of the service. The customer needs to control the versions of all interfacing systems along with all documents previously mentioned.

It is essential in every form of testing to know which software version and which test basis version is used. The use of services does not make this easier because the supplier will not always communicate all changes. As a result, an incorrect version of Web Service Description Language (WSDL) may be used as a basis for a mock service. For these reasons, the presence of version control is part of manageability testing.

5.4.8   Maintainability of software

Maintainability of application software is the responsibility of the customer (PaaS and IaaS) or the responsibility of the supplier (SaaS). Poor maintainability results in recurring errors and parts of the service not functioning after changes and patches. If this leads to significant issues, it may cause a customer to look for a different service (supplier). These errors in production are visible when users complain, in the continuous regression test, and from monitoring tools. Poor maintainability of the customer's in-house software is a reason to look for a cloud solution.

5.5 Availability/continuity testing

Availability and *continuity* are terms that can cause confusion when used next to each other. Availability is about a part of the IT landscape, such as a service. Continuity is about the process that uses it. Availability is a precondition for continuity. For instance, the continuity of the invoicing process depends on the availability of the email service to send invoices.

The continuity of processes is key (also known as business continuity and business reliability), and the following questions need to be answered: How often does a disruption occur, how fast is it resolved, and what damage has this disruption caused? To reach high service availability, a duplicated setup is needed so when a failure occurs, a spare part can take over the function of the failing part (failover or fallback). These mechanisms are (luckily) rarely used, so it is uncertain whether they actually work. However, the impact is large, so testing is crucial.

The service model determines the involvement of a customer. In SaaS, all layers of service hardware and software are within the supplier's black box. The way in which service availability is kept at a certain level is not visible to the customer. The supplier needs to map out what the impact is of losing the entire service and losing the connections to the service from other systems.

In PaaS and IaaS, the involvement of both the customer and the supplier is intertwined. When the supplier changes to a backup system in the case of a platform or infrastructure disruption, the question is how the customer's software reacts. This question is also true for connections to systems with software that runs in the cloud.

Because of the dependency on external parties, a customer needs to have a plan B (disaster recovery plan) that addresses the full and long-term failure of the service or the Internet connection. This is the case when certain processes need to keep running. In such cases, the customer needs to set up an alternative (manual) process for which external employees may need to be hired and, potentially, extra workspaces need to be set up. By process simulation, the chance for success of such a plan B will considerably increase.

When there is a continuity failure, it is usually the service failure that is considered. However, the continuity of business processes can also be disrupted when a supplier alters the behavior of the service. Sometimes these can be predicted by previously announced changes. However, it must be taken into account that the supplier does not always announce changes in a timely or sufficiently detailed manner. A periodical E2E regression test can show such changes, depending, of course, on the coverage of the regression test. With some luck, the change that has been detected in the regression test has not led to any problems in the business processes. When the regression test does not reveal incidents, it unfortunately does not guarantee that the service has not been modified.

In addition to changes in the service, other events can occur that cause continuity to be in jeopardy. In the selection and implementation stages, what-if scenarios can be worked out during risk analysis. For example, what happens to the data when a supplier or the customer goes bankrupt or when there is a business conflict? With major business risks, testing or simulating what-if scenarios is a measure to be considered.

The availability of the requesting environment is also part of E2E continuity. However, the assumption is made that replacing a machine that is down with another machine only has a limited impact on the continuity of the business process.

5.5.1 Failure Mode and Effect Analysis

An important step in preventing problems is to systematically analyze different kinds of failures and the effect they have on production. Applying Failure Mode and Effect Analysis (FMEA) is a way of performing this analysis. This method goes a lot further than testing. One can decide to set up monitoring tools and logs, a different architecture, or a plan B as preventative measures. Applying an FMEA can be quite laborious, and for that reason, it mainly only happens for business processes with a high risk of failure.

At a high level, FMEA is applied as follows (see Figure 5–12):

- Find possible failure modes (failing mechanisms) in the production situation.
- Determine possible causes of failing mechanisms.
- Determine the severity of possible (damaging) impact of the failure.
- Design measures to discover and prevent the failure.

Measures are aimed at preventing failure by taking away the cause of it, lowering the chance of it occurring, or decreasing the impact. The focus of FMEA overlaps with that of a product risk analysis (PRA). The focus of the PRA is, however, more limited because it is predominantly used as a basis for test measures. In practice, FMEA is an iterative process: first the most serious failing mechanisms are dealt with, then those that remain are reviewed, until a further investment in the FMEA process can no longer be justified by the limited severity of the residual failing mechanisms.

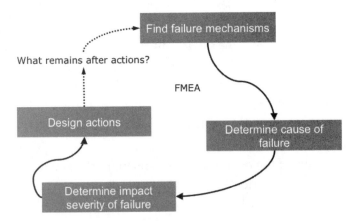

Figure 5–12 *FMEA process*

5.5.2   The role of architecture

Every part of the IT architecture has a likelihood of failure. The place in the IT architecture and the impact it has on the business process determines what impact the availability of the part has on the continuity of the business processes. With a model of the IT architecture and the (estimated) reliability of all components, one can calculate the reliability of an E2E chain. In highly critical processes, a cloud solution may not be able to offer the necessary level of business reliability. Calculating business reliability is a specialized profession, so we will not elaborate. But without calculations, the model can also be used for a qualitative reliability analysis by determining single points of failure and where duplicated setups are used. A single point of failure stops the business process when it fails. A power cut is a trivial example of this. In a duplicated setup, the spare setup takes over the function, guaranteeing business process continuity. Duplicate setups are an expensive measure, doubling costs.

Not all of the IT architecture is controlled by the customer. In SaaS, the service is a black box with a certain level of availability. It is difficult to identify single points of failure or duplicated setups. The way in which the resources and other systems from the customer are connected to the black box can be mapped out. It may be that the analysis raises questions, such as why there is only a single Internet connection at the customer side (single point of failure).

In PaaS and IaaS, the customer can map out the architecture. It should be known how the service supplier deals with failure of infrastructure or the platform. Think about activating a backup system, which is kept on standby. This backup system also needs to be included in the architecture map. In the overall mapping, one can start to find weak and strong points in the reliability chain. In IaaS and PaaS, all interfacing systems are, of course, part of the architecture map.

By deliberately causing a single point of failure, one can test a (possibly manual) backup scenario. Testing duplicated setups is described in section 5.5.8. Because failover changes (luckily) occur very infrequently, it is far from certain that the mechanism actually works when it is needed. Testing is no luxury given the investment in the duplicated setup.

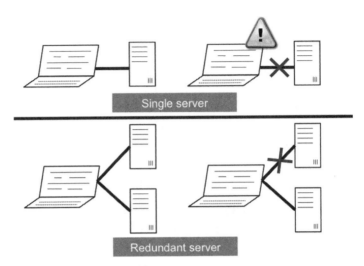

Figure 5-13   *Redundant server*

5.5.3   Hardware reliability

Some failures can be predicted by the customer by monitoring the condition of the platform and the infrastructure (with PaaS and IaaS). The customer presumably cannot access the hardware because they are separated by a virtualization layer. Nonetheless, monitoring virtual parts of the infrastructure does tell something about the proper functioning of the hardware on which the virtualization effectively runs.

An example of monitoring is measuring memory use. When the available memory depletes due to a software error, continuity can be threatened. The best thing is that this becomes visible even before an actual failure occurs. In addition, error messages and warnings are logged (for example, reading errors on the hard disk). When the number of reading errors in a time unit rises, the hard disk will probably break down in the near future and need to be replaced in a timely matter. In all cases, hardware reliability is the supplier's responsibility and not something for the customer to worry about.

By testing the monitoring tools and reviewing the logs, the supplier can reduce the risk that the tools won't function properly in practice. This can be done by simulating a problem (this is called fault seeding) and checking whether it is detected. In certain industries (for example, telecoms, aviation), special hardware versions are created that simulate a hardware error on command to determine whether the software is able to detect the degradation. When a customer wants to be able to monitor and log the platform or infrastructure, this needs to be taken into account as a selection criterion.

5.5.4 Software reliability

An important part of the continuity chain is the software reliability; that is, the degree to which the service runs without failure due to errors in the software itself. With SaaS, a distinct boundary exists: the quality of all software in the cloud is the responsibility of the supplier. The customer takes care of the software and interfacing systems that are not running in the cloud. With PaaS and IaaS, a part of the software belongs to the customer and a part belongs to the supplier. As far as the reliability of the customer's software, nothing changes when moving to the cloud.

Reliability of supplier software is an unknown. In part, this uncertainty can be removed by the customer performing functionality tests (see section 5.6). An understanding of the supplier's development process can also increase the confidence of the customer—for example, tests they perform, their programming standards, configuration management, and so on. A process audit is a suitable tool to increase understanding.

A specific characteristic of software (and therefore also of a service) is the robustness against unforeseen user actions (including errors). In other words, what is the chance that the business process continuity will be disrupted by the user?

Here are some examples of user actions that can cause SaaS error situations:

- Unexpected input (syntax test)
- Closing user interface without logging off
- Not working according to standard workflow (skipping steps, re-executing steps)
- Simultaneously performing conflicting actions on different resources
- Stopping actions in different places

The following user actions can cause PaaS error situations:

- Rolling out the wrong software (can it be reversed?)
- Accidentally throwing away files

These user actions can cause IaaS error situations:

■ Accidentally changing infrastructure
■ Rolling out the wrong operating system

5.5.5 Guarantees and SLAs

Guarantees

When the importance of availability is high (for instance, with a web shop), the availability of the service needs to be measured to determine whether the guaranteed levels are met. Suppliers usually guarantee a certain availability that feels quite high, such as 99.9 percent. In practice this means that the service can be offline for over eight hours per year and, with that, decimate the turnover of a peak day. Two conclusions can be drawn. First of all, the number of nines in the guarantee of availability can make the difference between acceptable and unacceptable. Second, the continuity of a business process can have a different risk profile at different times. For the purpose of performance testing, an operational profile is designed, which is a model of the measured or expected use, distributed over time. Such a profile is also a helpful reference in judging which periods are most relevant for continuity. In section 5.9, we discuss testing a service for the performance guaranteed by the supplier.

SLAs

In an SLA, a specific agreement may be made between a customer and a supplier about service availability. Availability is a key performance indicator (KPI). By reporting to the customer on the delivered availability, the supplier shows professionalism and quality of service. The customer monitors the continuity of the service itself in the E2E process (for instance, by keeping track of when users complain about the service failing). Based on this information, it can be determined whether this KPI is met or not. In addition to the fail frequency, there is another useful KPI, namely how fast a failure is resolved. Failure and repair time in an SLA are often described by the following metrics:

■ Mean time between failures (MTBF): how often a failure occurs.
■ Mean time to repair/recovery (MTTR): how long it takes, on average, to resolve the failure.

Points to note

Here are some points to note with regard to continuity guarantees:

- Determine what is meant exactly by up- and downtime. (For example, is regular maintenance considered downtime or not?)
- List which parties are involved. Are there other parties involved? For instance, if a SaaS supplier uses IaaS from another supplier for the infrastructure, the SaaS supplier has ultimate responsibility over the availability guarantees.
- Decide how to deal with failures outside the responsibility of the service supplier, such as Internet failures. In measuring service availability, this has to be taken into account
- Decide how to deal with failures in the interaction between resources on which support is not explicitly guaranteed by the supplier. In short, the boundary between customer and supplier responsibility needs to be sufficiently clear when availability is measured.

5.5.6   Impact of availability mechanisms

There are different mechanisms by which a service supplier can realize service availability to a certain level. Mirroring is a method that is often used, where a copy of the data, a machine, or even a complete (virtual) environment is kept available. This is shown in Figure 5–14. In the case of a failure, the mirror will be activated as a fallback. In many cases a disconnection of the service and data loss (since the last mirror synchronization process took place) has to be taken into account when switching to a fallback part.

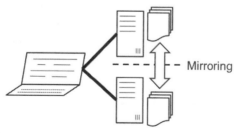

Figure 5–14   *Mirroring*

Failure is not the only reason services move from one location to another. This can also be part of the supplier's optimization strategy. A better use of servers (load balancing) or making room for elasticity in a certain location can, for example, be reasons to move services.

The service provider is responsible for guaranteeing the availability of the service, whether it is IaaS, PaaS, or SaaS. Fallback needs to be tested regularly by the service provider. Parts of the service that don't yet have active users may serve as a test environment.

When a customer wants to experience a supplier fallback to determine how it impacts E2E continuity in the business processes, it requires a great deal of alignment between customer and supplier.

5.5.7   Internet and Internet connection

The Internet itself has built-in redundancy (there is more than one route from A to B), but the degree of redundancy can vary widely from location to location. Holland, for example, is very well connected to the Internet because an important international Internet connection point is present in the country; South America has a limited number of physical routes to the rest of the Internet world. In certain countries the Internet is filtered selectively, and in other countries the Internet is less stable (there is an anecdote that tells of cable thieves shutting down the entire Internet connection of a nation). In short, the availability of the Internet can vary a lot in different countries. In most cases, that cannot be influenced by a potential customer and may be a reason not to bring company-critical processes to the cloud.

The connection of an organization to the Internet is part of the chain. The Internet connection is provided by a telecom provider. How are availability guarantees of Internet connections set up? For most consumers and small and medium-sized organizations, the connection to the Internet is an ADSL or DSL line, which seldom has a duplicated setup. When there are multiple connections to the Internet, the duplicated mechanism can also be tested. It is expected that service suppliers have a reliable (multiple) connection to the Internet available. An audit can judge whether this is the case.

Guarantees for continuity, therefore, need to be judged in the light of the supplier's and customer's locations. The supplier can be very well connected to the Internet and offer very high availability; the customer may be in a less favorable location. The risk of the Internet connection then lies with the customer.

5.5.8 Testing failover

With SaaS, there is not much to test for parts that are duplicated. At most the switch to a manual procedure (by the customer) when the service fails. The SaaS supplier has the most to test and can use the failover test procedure. The ultimate test in this case is a coordinated test between the customer and supplier in which the customer helps to determine whether the entire environment is identical after failover.

With PaaS and IaaS, in many cases there is interaction between the customer and supplier when the service fails. The customer can test this unilaterally, by simulating loss of service and testing how the in-house software responds. However, it is much better to test failover in collaboration with the service provider. When failover procedures are as easy as suppliers promise them to be, collaborating in a test with the supplier should not be a problem.

To test a failover, the starting point is a duplicated setup. One of the duplicated setup parts is dropped, the system switches to the spare part, and continuity is tested. There may be a calculated loss of data (repair is a part of service recovery), but it is possible that the IT architecture can be set up whereby no loss of data occurs when parts of the service fail.

Failover test cases

Follow these steps to test the continuity of the service with a duplicated setup (parts A and B):

1. Normal operation (A is active).
2. Part A is set to inactive (a disruption is detected, a switch is made).
3. Part B runs the service (the switch was successful).
4. Part A is set to active (normally, the service keeps using B).
5. Part B is set to inactive (a disruption is detected, a switch is made).
6. Part A runs the service (the switch was successful).
7. Part B is set to active (has no further effect).
8. Normal operation.
9. *Potentially a second test cycle.*

In Figure 5–15 a state transition diagram is shown in which all states and transitions in the failover switches are indicated. In it can be seen that the preceding steps listed pass only four transitions of a possible ten (the outer states are passed clockwise). When the need for continuity is very high (risk), all transitions need to be tested. The service supplier also has to comply with this procedure.

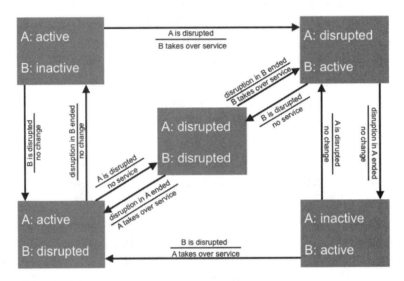

Figure 5–15   *Failover transitions*

When executing a failover test, the worst-case scenario is assumed: failure at a peak time. In any case, the service needs to be fully running to mimic a realistic situation. There needs to be work in progress so testing what happens with data during a failure can be done properly.

With a failover test, it is about showing that the interruption of a service stays within acceptable or agreed-upon boundaries. A failover is not finished entirely until the cause of failure is fixed and the original situation is recovered. The time a failure lasts comprises the following:

- The time it takes to detect the failure
- The time it takes to end the failure
- The time it takes to repair possible damage

Large environments are made up of hundreds of components. With very high business risks, it may be necessary to test the failure of many or most of these components one by one in the failover test (in individual failover test cases). Usually it suffices to include only the most crucial components in the failover test—not all failing components cause complete service disruption. Degradation can also occur (for instance, a lower performance because fewer servers are available).

Failover testing needs to be done on a production-like environment, such as, for instance, on an identical test environment from the cloud or in the production environment before a service is live.

Specific checkpoints in failover tests

Under the hood of a successful failover process, a number of things need to work properly:

- IP addresses are switched.
- Load balancers stop trying to connect to the failed processes.
- Backups are restored.
- Machines can be restarted after a power cut (every physical server, storage, load balancer, other equipment).
- Networks will be up and running after a failure (pulling cables).
- Other failures are repaired (every virtual machine, database server, interface).
- Data (or messages) is not lost or corrupted.
- Hardware or software that has failed or is stopped is automatically (recovery tools) or manually restarted.
- Procedures are followed that clearly describe who is responsible for what (calling support staff, escalation procedures).
- Operational support is provided by personnel and tools.
- Failures are analyzed.
- Log files are inspected.
- Failures are diagnosed.
- Backup systems are monitored.
- Possible damage (information that is lost) is repaired (damage control)—for instance, data is re-entered, transactions are restarted.

The preceding points are especially applicable to IaaS but less so to PaaS. For SaaS and PaaS, there are additional points to note.

The following checklist is for SaaS continuity after failover switch:

- Has the configuration been disturbed?
- Is the failure even noticed?
- Does the automatic failover start to work?
- Are there any transactions lost?
- Is there any data lost (counts, checksums)?
- If there is an audit trail, does it function properly?
- Is performance back to normal?
- Are there any incidents from the functional regression test (perhaps a limited set, for instance aimed at the fifty most used or most vital functions)?

A useful test technique is the data cycle test (for example, testing create, read, update, and delete [CRUD] actions before and after the failover).

The PaaS checklist for after a failover switch is as follows:

- Is it still possible for the customer to roll out new software?
- Is the platform software running again?
- Is the platform development environment active again?

The checklists are indicative only. The boundaries between SaaS, PaaS, and IaaS and the responsibilities of the customer and supplier for executing checks, in practice, are not that distinct.

Test management aspects for failover tests

Here are some points to note for the successful execution of failover tests:

- Sufficient technical support is needed from different disciplines. Finding the cause of a failure possibly requires in-depth knowledge of the technique and the log files.
- Sufficient functional knowledge of the E2E processes is needed. How do service, infrastructure, or platform failures translate to problems in the customer's business processes? How can dependency possibly be decreased?
- Before a failover test is started, all planned service tests need to be completed so with the failover only related errors are found (failover tests are expensive).
- As with any test, the right authorizations in the services involved are needed.

▓ With a coordinated failover test, the supplier needs to be willing to cooperate.

Process simulation

Failover procedures can also be tested by means of process simulation. A catastrophe is enacted and all procedures and manuals are run through. This is highly suitable for relevant personnel to gain experience (and the risk of an unnecessarily long outage of the service is decreased).

5.5.9 Testing working offline

The impact of a failure on the availability of a service is strongly influenced by the degree to which working offline is possible. This is, for instance, the case when (part of) the data is available on the user side and, when online, is synchronized with the service. Examples are Exchange email and Dropbox.

When a difference arises between the local situation and the cloud situation, this can lead to problems (and with that, threaten the continuity of the business processes).

Here are some examples:

▓ Work continues, based on out-of-date information, and this information could be changed in the cloud during the offline period.

▓ The users are not aware that they are working (partly) online (and are lead to believe differently).*

▓ Synchronization conflicts arise because data is changed locally as well as in the cloud.

* *A specific example. A user was traveling and used Dropbox. The icon in the Taskbar showed that Dropbox was fully synchronized, but the changes in the cloud were still not updated locally due to a limitation with the Internet connection.*

We suggest the following test cases from a continuity standpoint:

- End the connection and check whether the users can see that they are working offline.
- Disrupt the connection (for instance, a port or a certain type of IP traffic) and check whether problems arise.
- Check whether changes that are made offline find their way to the cloud when online status is regained.
- Check whether conflicts between offline and cloud data are handled robustly (which is in fact a functional requirement).

5.6 **Functionality testing**

Acquiring SaaS can, in terms of functionality, be compared to buying software packages. There is a standard service that is provided and it has to fit in the intended processes in one way or another. The functionality of platform (PaaS) or infrastructure (IaaS) services is in an entirely different league than that of SaaS. The PaaS user group is to be found in the development department that uses the platform in the cloud for different environments and the department that rolls out the in-house software and keeps it operational. IaaS users are people that configure the infrastructure in the cloud, roll out software on the infrastructure, and keep the environment operational. This is traditionally a task for the data center.

Just as with testing packages, a number of different test objectives can be determined. For a start, a standard service usually does not fit exactly to the business processes that are going to use it. Flexible services can be configured to match the business processes. Customization is needed when no further configuration is possible and the match to the business processes is not yet completed. But where should the customization take place? Is the supplier going to expand the service or modify it for a certain customer or group of customers (for instance, for a community cloud)? Or is the customer going to make the changes, for instance, to connect the service to other systems? Test activities for both cases are required and are discussed in this chapter. In addition to changing the service, it may be decided to also change the business processes. A strong argument can be put forward for these changes when standard processes such as email, CRM, Electronic Patient Dossier (EPD, health care), and policy administration are in place, not only from the perspective of one-time development costs, but certainly also from an administration point of view (think of upgrades).

The software quality of a service is the supplier's responsibility, and they have to go through a proper software development process to make sure customers do not suffer from defects in the software. As a result, it is not the primary task of customers to test software quality or service stability. However, because of the business risks, a customer still needs to perform an acceptance test on the service for critical parts of the business process. The outcome will weigh heavily on the selection decision.

There are a number of functional test objectives:

- Does the service fit the business processes?
- Do the business processes fit the service?
- Is the service quality sufficient (number of bugs)?
- Is the service sufficiently user friendly?
- Is the service configuration done correctly?
- Does potential supplier customization function properly?
- Does potential customer customization function properly?
- Do interfaces between the service and other systems work properly?
- Are platforms that are relevant to the customer being properly supported?
- Does everything work after changes (is there no regression)?

These and a number of other test objectives are translated in this section into test strategies. The approach in this section targets primarily SaaS functionality, but we also provide handles for test managers who have to scrutinize IaaS or PaaS functionality.

To create and execute test cases, a test basis is needed. It is unlikely that for all functional test objectives in the preceding list, designs exist with sufficient detail to deduct test cases. To be able to perform useful tests, one will need to gather additional information. This is also discussed in this section.

5.6.1   Compatibility of service with business processes

To what extent does the service fit the business processes? This is similar to the objective of a user acceptance test (UAT). It seems fitting to choose a similar approach. Not only is the service itself the test object, but also manuals and possibly accompanying courses are part of it. The starting point is the business or user processes. If there are no descriptions of them available, these need to be generated. Based on process descriptions, test scenarios can be defined using the process cycle test (PCT) technique.

In a PCT, a flowchart is needed as the test basis (see Figure 5–16). With the simplest PCT variant, all paths in the flowchart are run through once (this is called test depth level one). Every path, from the top to the bottom of the flowchart, is a test case. The expected result of each test case is that the path can be followed. From process descriptions in the form of use cases, flowcharts can easily be produced. On these flowcharts, a PCT can also be run. A stronger variation of the PCT (test depth level two) can be considered for parts of the process for which it is important that all combinations of entering and exiting a decision point are tested (high risk).

In many cases, the business process will go through a number of connected systems, of which the service becomes a part. This means that it is not enough to test the service alone. The E2E business processes need to be run from start to finish. For this, the process descriptions are used as the test basis. To determine which parts need to be run, the classification tree technique can be used.

As an increasing amount of business process components are brought to the cloud, the customer will need to integrate different services in the IT landscape. As a result, it becomes more important to check E2E to confirm whether all these services communicate properly with each other.

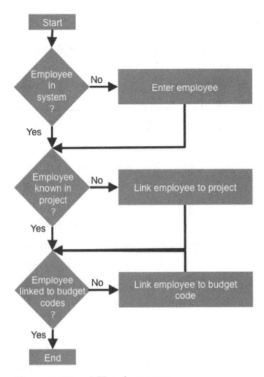

Actor: project secretary
Preconditions: logged on; one or more
budget codes can be linked

Basic flow:
-   open project screen
-   select employee
-   select budget code
-   link employee to budget code

Alternative flow 1:
employee unknown in system
→ use case: add employee

Alternative flow 2:
employee unknown in project
→ use case: link to project

Post-conditions: employee is linked to all
necessary budget codes

Figure 5–16   *PCT and use cases*

5.6.2   Testing service quality

A customer can perform an acceptance test on the service to get an impression
of service quality. Test scenarios are designed and executed for the most important processes for which the service will be used. Additionally, in some areas of
the service more detailed tests are executed. When the results are error free, it
gives a good impression of the service quality. (See also the discussion of software reliability in section 5.5.4.) Achieving well-defined test coverage is not an
objective in itself when the customer measures the service quality. Because of
that, exploratory testing is a useful approach. In testing service quality, functionality can be interpreted widely. One can also form an opinion on the service's user-friendliness. Prior to testing, criteria need to be designed for the
nonfunctional requirements that are tested implicitly (for instance, "a maximum of two screens are needed to make an appointment").

In exploratory testing, the service is divided into segments, and each segment is allocated an amount of time for testing. The division into segments is based on risk (the parts with higher risk initially get more test time). For each segment an assignment is created for what needs to receive special attention (for instance, screen handling, speed, accuracy, stability). The test for each segment will be time boxed, and within the time box, the tester starts to design a number of test cases. This will be based on the assignment and on information about the workings of that service segment. The test cases are executed immediately. When the test result is according to expectations, the tester continues with testing the segment, to a depth such that the entire segment can be evaluated during the available time box. When the test result is not according to expectations, the tester can decide to zoom in on the problem and locally test deeper with the use of error guessing (often there is more going on; software defects have a tendency to cluster). When the time box is ended, a decision needs to be made. When testing did not result in issues, the testing of the segment is completed and tests for the next segment can be started. When there are issues (such as found defects), an extra time box may be needed to finish examining that segment. When a defect is severe enough, possible rejection of that segment follows. It can also be the case that an extra time box is assigned to testing the segment around the problem area and in areas that have not been covered sufficiently. When all planned segments are tested, the results are summarized: are the results satisfactory and is there any reason to doubt the quality of the service?

When there is functionality in the service that is especially critical to the business process, the customer can decide to use other test techniques in order to get a clear understanding of the software quality of that functionality.

What exactly is the test basis for this test activity? The customer does not have the functional design available because that is a document internal to the supplier. The necessary information will be found in manuals and course materials. As part of an exploratory test, the tester continuously needs to determine the expected result, based on assumptions and previous experience.

5.6.3 Testing user-friendliness

In addition to basic service quality and how the software fits the business processes, user-friendliness is important. The support it receives from users is a significant factor. When it is clear what user-friendliness means to an organization

(How many screens does a user have to go through to make an appointment? Is the tab order sufficiently intuitive? Is there sufficient help functionality?), this can be incorporated implicitly or explicitly in the functional test activities. When user-friendliness is difficult to specify, but it is important to involve end users, one has to let the end users work with the service in a test environment and learn their findings afterward. A manual or work instructions (user documentation) can act as a test basis and at the same time be a test object: all flaws are findings.

User documentation

When testing user documentation that is written by the supplier, a tester usually reviews the quality of the document (well written, spell checked, etc.) and whether it is in accordance with how the software works. In testing manuals for services, the test focus will be on checking whether the manual corresponds with practical use. The instructions in the manual are executed and tested for comprehensiveness (for the intended user), for completeness (all steps described), and for correctness (is it right). Section 5.4.3 contains more information on user documentation.

5.6.4   Testing interfaces to other systems

In many cases, interfaces between the service and other systems are used (see Figure 5–17)—for instance, invoicing in the cloud, for which customer data needs to be uploaded from the internal CRM system. In testing interfaces, four aspects are differentiated:

- **The technique.** How is data exchange organized physically (for instance, a comma-separated value [CSV] file or XML)?
- **The syntax.** How are data structured and what are the syntax rules? For instance, is it structured by using XML Schema Documentation (XSD) for XML messages or a definition for a CSV file?
- **Semantics.** Are uploaded or downloaded data processed correctly by the receiving service or receiving system?
- **Nonfunctional aspects (such as security and performance).** Any problems in these areas?

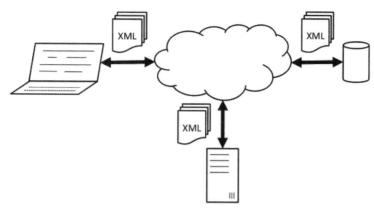

Figure 5–17 *Interfaces with the cloud*

Testing for the first aspect is implicitly integrated in the next two. Testing the syntax is about the number of (optional and mandatory) fields, the order in which the fields are arranged, and for each field, which values are valid and which are not. Information from the sending system needs to be tested to determine whether it matches that of the receiving system. Well-known problems are related to date formats that do not match, decimals, text versus numerical data, number ranges, field lengths, special characters (@#$%^&*(), "), "standard" XML interfaces that prove to be less than standard, and so on. Testing for semantics can best be combined with testing the E2E process (see section 3.1.3). The focus of testing interfaces is in testing with data that can occur in real life (and not, per se, the testing of the service).

The test basis for testing interfaces comprises interface specifications. There are many (including open source) test tools available that can be used for testing interfaces. After loading an XSD or WSDL file, (see section 5.6.8) test cases that need to be executed on the interfaces can be generated automatically.

Incidents between interfaces need to be solved because otherwise the E2E process does not function. The customer and supplier need to negotiate to determine which side should solve the incident. When a supplier cannot be contacted, the customer needs to work on a workaround, in the form of customization, for instance (an adapter or bridge).

5.6.5   Testing service configuration

The use of services in business processes usually requires a certain amount of configuration. Incorrect configuration can result in a system that does not function as desired. Before the customer uses the service, analysis is needed to determine what needs to be configured for the service. Here are some examples:

- Configuring authorizations
- (Possibly) configuring the workflow
- Configuring several general options (language, communication protocols, date formats)
- Configuring look and feel (company style, company colors, logos)
- Detailed configuration of the service (what is used, what is not, mandatory fields)

The scope and depth of testing the configuration depends on the risks that coincide with use. The following can go wrong:

- Design of the configuration is incorrect (ill-conceived).
- There are configuration errors.
- Service configuration does not work properly.
- General setup prevents the service from working properly.

For the first item a review is necessary. For the second item a test by the configuration specialist is a necessary first step (in fact, a unit or component test), which also involves testing the third item. An option for increasing test depth is for a check to be made by a configuration specialist colleague (a collegial test).

A system test of the configuration with formal test techniques is a very extreme measure and not always necessary, and it's not always done in software packages. If the risk is high (the impact of incorrect configuration is very high), one can execute a system test using formal functional test techniques on the configuration, such as an elementary comparison test (ECT), a decision table test, or a test using a classification tree (also known as a data combination test).

Testing general configurations and look-and-feel should not be skipped. In packages, carelessness in configuration leads to large failures in functionality. This can also happen with services.

5.6.6 Customization by the supplier

When a supplier customizes a service for all customers, in effect a new version of the service is created. Depending on the risks associated with the changes, the customer can choose from the different options for test strategies, described in this chapter.

With changes for one or a limited number of customers, the question is how thoroughly the supplier has tested the modifications. A modification for a specific customer (in contradiction of the essence of the cloud) will require an acceptance test by the customer. The appropriate test techniques need to be chosen based on the characteristics of the changed part of the service. Testing also includes a connections test and an E2E test, to a depth commensurate with the risks.

Incidents that occur as a result of customization by the supplier need to be solved by the supplier.

5.6.7 Customization by the customer

Custom modifications on the customer side need to be tested by the customer. The developer executes unit and system tests, and an acceptance test, including an interface test and an E2E test, is then performed by the customer. Examples of custom modifications on the customer side are adapters to translate files or messages in the service connection or a user interface to communicate with the service. The test basis consists of the customer's requirements and specifications.

Incidents need to be solved by the developer.

5.6.8 Testing web services

The World Wide Web Consortium (W3C), an international standardization organization for the World Wide Web, defines a web service as follows: "A software system designed to support interoperable machine-to-machine interaction over a network." In practice, a web service is a piece of software in which the functionality is accessible using standardized web protocols. The communication with a web service is via XML messages/files. A web service is usually accessible over the Internet and thus can be considered SaaS. Web services also are used as building blocks for SaaS. Testing a web service normally is part of the test program of the organization moving to the cloud.

Functional testing of web services can be done in a fairly standardized way. If it is clear what the service needs to be able to do, the traditional test case determination activity is performed.

WSDL

WSDL is the standard for describing the following items:

- The location (a URL) where the web service can be found
- The supported protocols
- The operations that the service can perform (in a library service, for example, search for title, search for author, make a reservation)
- The structure of the messages used in communication with the web service

A WSDL file therefore contains the information on the technical design of the service. With the help of the WSDL, valid messages can be determined and the web service tested. SOA test tools are able to automatically determine test messages, send them to a web service, and judge whether valid messages are received from the web service. With a WSDL file, it is also possible to validate messages from other systems that are to be sent to the web service. Another option for the WSDL file is to create mock objects that simulate the messages from the web service. In the absence of a WSDL file there may be XSD that defines the message interaction with the web service.

Note that the WSDL file and the web service sometimes contradict each other. By executing compliancy tests, it will become clear whether the web service is implemented according to the technical design. When an error occurs, the WSDL file or the web service may be the cause.

Tools

Although web services can be tested manually, it is not efficient and therefore not recommended. Creating XML messages is a very error-prone and time-consuming task. There are a number of tools (both open source and commercial) that offer support for creating messages. In addition, the communication protocol generally requires advanced functionality, such as adding SOAP headers with encryption. This is not doable without test tools.

Test cases

As an intake on a web service, all possible operations of the service need to be requested once. When the service responds to every request and the answer indicates that each operation exists, functional testing can start.

In designing test cases for (web) services, distinguish between test cases with regard to the message structure and test cases that are about functionality. Note that when you are using tools, generally only valid message structures are generated. To determine how the service performs in fault handling, it is necessary to define incorrect messages not only based on content but also based on structure.

When different environments (or mocks) are used, it is important to check how the message is addressed. It often happens that the wrong incident (or no incident at all) is raised, due to the fact that messages weren't addressed correctly.

5.6.9   Multi-platform testing

One of the main advantages of working in the cloud is the opportunity to access the service using different resources. In addition to the new technology that makes this possible, two other coinciding trends have arisen. These are the New World of Work and the BYOD phenomenon. With the New World of Work, the working location is not, per se, bound to the office and people increasingly work outside office hours. This requires access to the IT facilities over the Internet. More and more people like to work with their own equipment rather than with the resources made available to them by their employer. Laptops, tablets, and smartphones are in this category. Testing different combinations of platforms and services is summarized here under the term *multi-platform testing*.

Which variations can be applicable (see Figure 5–18)?

- Browser types (IE, Safari, Chrome)
- Variations of apps
- Different operating systems (Windows, iOS, Linux, etc.)
- Different mobile devices (tablets, smartphones)
- Different versions of hardware

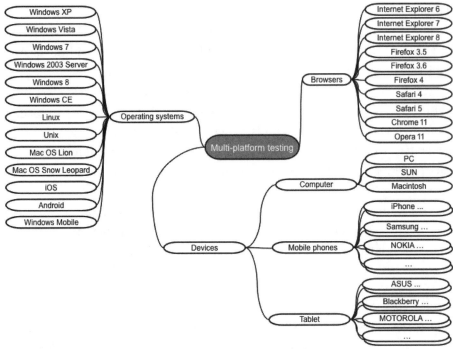

Figure 5–18   *Possible variations*

Considerations for the supplier

It is in the interest of the supplier to test the service with common platforms (portability test). A complete functional test per platform is not feasible. There are choices to be made. There are a number of considerations on which to base choices:

■ User statistics. Which platforms and versions are used the most?

■ New platforms. A supplier may want its profile connected with supporting a new platform that is not yet found in user statistics.

■ Platforms that share the same kernel. Testing one platform per kernel can be sufficient to cover the most important risks.

■ Focusing on the most-used paths through the service.

■ Testing one of each kind of technical facility (client-side scripts, forms, media, control types).

■ Different technical facilities in apps (global positioning system (GPS)/no GPS, camera/no camera, Wi-Fi/no Wi-Fi).

■ Requesting all screens and menus once.

When the supplier follows W3C web standards closely in designing and building services and makes no or little use of specific properties and possibilities of platforms, portability risk is limited.

Testing the multitude of mobile devices is becoming a problem. In section 3.3, an example of test services that respond to this is described.

Considerations for the customer

A customer has different choices to make. Defining a BYOD policy is in most organizations still in its early stages. In this policy, a number of matters need to be defined. This leads to determining the following categories:

- The standard office setups used within the organization
- Other resources that are supported (for instance certain types of mobile devices)
- Resources that are allowed to be used but are not guaranteed
- Resources that are not allowed to be used

The first and second categories are fully incorporated in the multi-platform test. For the third category, a sample can be applied to testing, or it is not incorporated in the test strategy at all. The fourth category is outside the scope, except when an organization wants to test if the "forbidden platforms" are denied. In determining what needs to be tested, the same considerations apply as for the supplier.

5.6.10 Testing of and testing with apps

In practice, there is more and more mobile access to IT services. The access to services can be through the browser of mobile devices, but one uses special apps to address a service. These apps can be supplied by the service supplier (mostly cost free), but apps developed by other parties are also offered. What does this mean for testing?

An app that a supplier has developed in-house has to be tested over the Internet with the service in a system integration test (of course, the app itself also has to be tested!). When a customer wants to use the app, it is incorporated in the test activities that are part of the service test strategy. When a customer wants to use a different app, the customer is the system integrator and will have to execute a system integration test (depending on the risk and the importance of the app).

Testing an app (on a mobile device)

Testing an app is similar to testing traditional applications. There are, however, a number of extra points to note. With the use of mobile devices, for example, less storage space, less memory, and failing Internet connections need to be considered. In addition, the standard functionality of the mobile devices may affect the use of the app—for example, incoming calls, connecting or disconnecting battery chargers, locking the screen, and in many cases, a touch screen.

For most mobile platforms, simulators are available that can support testing apps on different combinations of mobile devices and operating systems. Because these simulators are also used by suppliers of mobile devices, it is likely that all capabilities of the devices are incorporated in the simulator. In addition to testing the app on a simulator, it needs to be tested on (a selection of) actual devices. In testing apps, there are different stakeholders: the app supplier, the app customer, and the end users. These need to be included in the app testing strategy.

There is another aspect to testing apps that are sold through a store: the store places a number of added requirements on the apps, such as making sure phone data is secure. All requirements of the store need to be incorporated in the entire development process and therefore also in testing. When this is not done properly, the store will not approve the app and the app will not be offered.

5.6.11 Testing for working offline

The ability to work offline is an important feature of many services. It is possible to keep working during the (temporary) absence of a connection to a service. At the moment that the connection is recovered, the synchronization process that takes place when the connection is recovered needs to be tested. In section 5.5.9, the test approach for testing working offline is described in more detail.

5.6.12 Testing for regression

When something changes in the IT landscape (the service or something else), there is always the chance that not everything is working correctly. When changes take place, consideration needs to be given to where and how extensive regression tests should be. Regression testing is mostly likely to be performed on functionality, but degradation also occurs in other areas (for instance, performance). Nonfunctional aspects can be included implicitly in a functional regression test. Determining whether everything still works is, of course, not a feasible objective. The risk analysis will determine the depth of testing.

5.6.13 Creating a test basis

A supplier is supposed to follow a regular software development process. The supplier can use the functional specifications as a basis for testing the service. For customers, things are different. A service is not chosen based on a functional design because it is about more or less standard functionality. Chances are high that the service and the business process meet for the first time in the testing stage. This will be the first time the service is checked in detail to ascertain whether there is a proper fit. For a test manager or tester to be able to prepare for that with test scenarios, a certain test basis is needed. In many cases, not many of the business processes are documented.

There are different ways to model the desired use of the service. The end users or qualified representatives are the most important people to speak to for creating the models. The more detailed the models need to be, the more time and effort it takes. The desired level of detail needs to be determined based on the risk profile of the modelled processes. A business analyst can provide their services to the test team at this point.

Following is a summary of a number of techniques to determine the test basis.

Process flows

To determine whether a certain way of working is even possible with a service, a process model is drawn up, with activities and decision points. This is an excellent starting point for a PCT. With a process model, the business process is key. The model predominantly targets the flow through the process and not so much the detailed functionality. Process flows normally will not stop at the boundaries of the service but cover the entire E2E process. As a result, they are also the test basis for the E2E test. It is often not until the process flows are worked out that it becomes clear whether the processes are completely defined. Exceptions will often be documented here for the first time.

Use cases

Creating use cases is similar to creating process flows, only here the user is key. By connecting all use cases, the entire business process can be covered. In a use case, there is the opportunity to describe detailed functionality. The degree of detail again depends on the risk profile. From a use case, if done right, a process model can also be determined and serve as a test basis for a PCT. Detailed functionality can be worked out using another test technique when desired.

Here are the important parts of a use case:

- **Actors**. Who or what is executing this use case?
- **Preconditions**. What needs to be configured before the use case can be executed?
- **Triggers**. Which action or actions initiate this use case?
- **Basic flow**. These are the steps that make up the normal functionality of this use case.
- **Alternative flow**. These steps also can occur with this use case but deviate from the basic flow.
- **Post-conditions**. What has changed after executing the use case, or what is the expected result?
- **Cohesion between use cases**. This includes relationships to other use cases, so that when a change in a use case occurs, the impact on other parts of the system or on the environment is clear.

Classification tree

A classification tree (or data combination test) can be used to model the different variations in scenarios that all need to be processed by the service (see Figure 5–19). This is very suitable as a test basis for E2E tests, but it does also run through the process flows with different scenarios. Together with experts, the variations to be tested are determined. The classifications provide instant test cases.

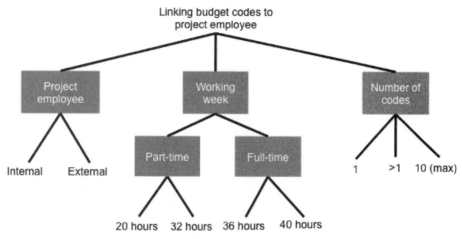

Figure 5–19 *Example of a classification tree*

CRUD

As services often support administrative processes, it is important to take creating, reading, updating, and deleting data into account. In the cloud, where others may also have access to data, it is important that all options are supported. Using a CRUD table with the most important kinds of data, it can be determined whether all desired options are present in the service. This technique is also applicable to testing authorization (which role can do what in the CRUD table).

Authorization table

Who is allowed to do what? *Who* might be a person, a role, or someone from a group. *What* could be access to certain data (CRUD) or access to certain parts of the service. To create a detailed enough authorization table, the service's options need to be taken into account. The authorization table is the test basis for the authorization tests (and implicitly for the authentication tests).

Interface specifications (agreements)

Interface specifications indicate how communication between the service and other systems will take place. The specifications describe the information structure that is exchanged, along with the field definitions. Increasingly, communication between systems uses XML. Specifications for XML files are often in

XSD files. With web services, the interface specifications are recorded in a WSDL, which should be provided by the web service supplier. In all specifications, information needs to be available about the following:

- Field structure
- Field names
- Mandatory and optional fields
- Field types
- Field lengths

Interface specifications are not obtained or created with the users, but with technical experts. The service supplier will have to deliver specifications with regard to connecting with the service. In a web service this is essential: without interface specifications, the web service is useless.

5.7 **Testing migration**

When an organization is going to use a service for an existing business process, a migration process is necessary. This will also be needed when use of a service ends—for instance, in case of switching to another supplier. This can be planned, but also unplanned (contract termination, bankruptcy).

The discussion of migration in this section mainly concerns data transfer. Data in this case means information. In a migration, there are a number of scenarios:

- Transfer into the cloud, where the applications remain the same (can be done with IaaS or PaaS). The data is only moved to another location.
- Transfer to SaaS. The data from the existing application needs to be migrated to the new service.
- Transfer from one SaaS to another SaaS. This will show a lot of similarities to the second scenario.
- Transfer out of the cloud. In most cases this will also mean a full data migration, similar to the second scenario.

In addition to simple migrations where data is transferred without change, data conversion is frequently needed. The data structures of the new environment are different from those of the original environment, which means that rules need to be drawn up to convert the data. Another special case of migration is synchronizing between the existing environment and the service. Both environments in this case are running in parallel.

5.7.1 Migration test strategy

The migration test strategy is directly linked to the migration strategy. Testing has the objective of lowering the risks related to a migration. The following general acceptance criteria for data migration function as a basis for the migration test objectives.

A successful migration can be described as follows:

- Interruption to business processes is minimal.
- All migrated data can be tracked (audit trail).
- All data is converted correctly.
- All transactions that were pending before migration are successfully completed after the migration (or finished before migration takes place).
- Defects in data before migration do not lead to problems during migration.
- Defects in data are solved and not migrated in their defective state (optional requirement).
- No more data than necessary is migrated to the service (no unnecessary data, no sensitive information unintentionally migrated).

Example. For the migration of an email service to the cloud, tools are usually available to migrate existing emails to the cloud environment. When the risks are not too high, testing is done by migrating one or some mailboxes and executing a limited number of tests on the result. For instance, testing could be done by means of a number of use cases: reading, forwarding, and replying with a limited check on contents. When that goes well for a number of mailboxes, implementation follows.

The business and legal importance of email is increasing and, as a result, so too is the importance of a correct migration. Migration tools in this case are to be subjected to a dedicated test.

The following possible migration test objectives (for the migration tool as well as for the migrated emails) should be considered:

- *Are any emails lost?*
- *Is the formatting of the emails unchanged (font, breaks, etc.)?*
- *Are any attachments lost?*
- *Can attachments still be opened?*
- *Are all other attributes migrated (priorities, flags, reply indicator)?*
- *Are dates and times of emails still correct?*

5.7.2 Minimal interruption of business processes

The migration to the service should interrupt the business processes as little as possible. After migration to the service, it is necessary to perform a check on the proper functioning of the service. This test targets the risks of service disruption caused by migrated data.

The test depth depends on the following factors:

- How robust is the service for unexpected contents in the imported data (is there a proper import check)?
- How important is the migrated data for the proper functioning of the service?
- How extensive are the changes in the way in which data is used?

The following needs to be tested:

- The most important business processes. To do this, process-oriented test cases are needed, tuned to the (possibly altered) user process.
- The correct import of data (is the data profile correct?).
- The potentially changed way in which data is used.
- The correct build-up of data history (correct order, with correct date and time).
- Vulnerable aspects, such as letter accents.

Trial migration

When the risks of migration and the importance of a correctly functioning system after migration are high, executing a trial migration might be considered. The steps described earlier are then executed in a test environment, with migrated production data.

5.7.3   Correct data migration in IaaS and PaaS

It is possible that the data is moved with the hardware, as is the case when setting up a private cloud. In this scenario, there is no real migration and there is nothing specific to test. E2E and regression tests do need to be executed. This is further elaborated on in section 5.6.

When there is new infrastructure but the data is copied to the cloud, a test needs to be executed to make sure the data transfers correctly to the target environment (for instance, with a checksum or a comparison of files in the old and new environment). Even when data structures do not change, surprises in the content can occur. An example of this is a problem that arises in date and time formats during the transfer to an environment where the country settings are different (month-day-year versus day-month-year).

5.7.4   Correct data conversion with SaaS

In a migration to SaaS, invariably a data conversion is needed. A strategy to do this is to fully rebuild the data by using the new (SaaS) application to manually enter the data. In most cases, however, this will be too labor intensive and error prone, and there will be a need for a tool to transfer data. This can be either a tool that is offered by the service supplier or custom-built conversion software (see Figure 5–20).

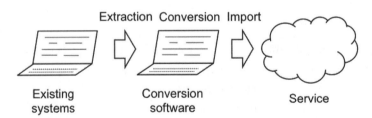

Figure 5–20   *Steps in migration*

Some migration test objectives are described next, along with the accompanying test approach for the conversion software.

Do conversion rules work correctly?

The most important check of conversion programs is an inspection beforehand of all rules for the data conversion. For designing dynamic test cases for the conversion, a number of techniques can be applied, such as equivalence classes, boundary values (valid/nonvalid range, input and output domain), and syntax tests in general (for instance, testing text fields that need to be converted to numeric fields). There might also be a need for semantic tests; there are scenarios in which data fields are mandatory, depending on the value in another field. The following aspects can be tested:

- Rounding, number of decimals (by rounding, totals are incorrect)
- Field lengths (which means that data may be truncated)
- Totals (columns and rows totals need to add up to the same total)
- Date and time conversions (08-09-11 can mean 8 September 2011 but possibly can be interpreted as 9 August 2011)

Does the conversion work properly on the input data?

An important option to build confidence in the conversion software is to execute one or more trial conversions with a representative set of data that is to be converted. In putting together a representative set (often real production data), cases that are representative of a large percentage of the data are needed, and also cases that are critical to the business processes (with large consequential damage when migration problems occur).

Is there any data lost?

With high-risk data (for instance, financial data), it is extremely important that there is no data lost or corrupted. Legislation and regulations might require that the migration route is controlled with an audit trail so that the integrity of the data can be demonstrated and all data manipulation during the migration is traceable. To create an audit trail, a representative and traceable quantity is chosen. Using checksums (for instance, the total amount of money) and data counts (for instance, persons or records), you can check whether data is lost during migration. Checksums and counts only provide an indication. Additional samples are needed to check the correctness of the data.

The audit trail needs to be functionally tested in advance, with a migration, to make sure the audit trail does the following:

- Confirms that the migration is executed correctly
- Detects any problems in the migration (all deviations and data not migrated need to be explained)

Are any partially completed transactions lost?

Migrations often take place while business processes are running. There can be transactions underway that need to be completed after the migration. One test objective is to ensure that a transaction that was underway prior to the migration can be successfully completed after the migration. Based on the work process or operational profiles, a set of transactions can be set up and tested in a trial migration. The need for a representative set and the severity of product risks (likelihood of failing and impact) determine the size and scale of the transaction migration test.

During and after conversion, does any sensitive data remain available?

Intermediate results are stored during the conversion, so the security measures during migration need to be similar to those of production. When the environment on which the conversion software is deployed is released after the conversion, no conversion data is allowed to remain behind on the environment. If the conversion software crashes, unwanted data can remain. By executing some tests on the behavior of the conversion software in the case of a crash, this risk is covered.

After a successful migration, the source systems can be shut down. Erasing the original data is also part of the privacy solution. This needs to be part of the migration strategy and therefore also be tested.

Is too much data being transferred to the service through migration?

Systems sometimes provide more data to another system than is strictly necessary. When all data stays in-house, that is not a problem. As soon as the information goes outside the company, checks are needed to ensure that no additional data is transferred to the service during the migration than is needed and allowed. This to prevent the leak of sensitive information. When applying migration tools that are provided by the service supplier, this just might happen.

It can be detected by inspection of the data designs of the source system and target service (and with that an inspection of the functioning of the supplier's migration tool).

Example. With migrating personal data to SaaS, it is intended that only the personal data ends up in the new service. There are examples in which other related data, such as data on wages and sick days, is included and placed in, for example, a Notes field (see Figure 5–21).

Figure 5–21   *Don't migrate too much*

5.7.5 Migration performance

When a lot of data needs to be migrated, a performance test is needed on the conversion software and also on the extraction from the source system and import into the service. A number of aspects are key here:

- **Speed**. Amount of processed data per time unit (there is a limited time window available for the migration in which the extraction from the source system, the conversion, and the import into the service has to take place).
- **Infrastructure capacity**. Is there, for instance, sufficient disk space to store intermediate results?
- **Stability at full volume**. There are no memory errors in using the conversion software or other situations that risk the conversion stability at full speed.

With trial migrations, the performance of the migration steps can be tested. The amount of data can be so large that in the first rounds of the trial migration only part of the data can be migrated. Performance data cannot be extrapolated directly for larger amounts of data, but can provide an indication. A trial migration on full speed remains necessary as a final test.

With conversion of large volumes, cloud computing can also offer a solution by using temporary processing facilities from the cloud, so the performance doesn't have to be a bottleneck.

5.7.6   Data cleanup

The (bad) condition of the input data can negatively affect the functioning of the conversion software. Moreover, people want to start with a clean slate in a new system and a new service. Therefore, data is cleaned up frequently prior to the conversion. To test the data cleanup, the conversion software can provide a good service, especially when it generates informative messages for erroneous input. When the conversion software is tested and approved, the entire set of production data to be cleaned up can be migrated. The error messages point to data that needs to be cleaned up. This data is corrected and the trial conversion can be restarted. When the conversion software contains only limited error detection, it may be necessary to develop a special data cleanup tool to detect the errors.

5.7.7   Test environment migration

Most attention in migrations is paid to data migration. But the migration to a new test environment should also be considered. Here are some points to note:

- Transfer and migrate test data (the same steps as with production data).
- Configure interfaces to other test systems.
- Organize access to the new environments.
- Configure administration for the new test environments (in test environments from the cloud, this is done by the supplier).
- Test the test environment (intake).

The new test environment can play an important role in migration—for instance, for executing trial migrations.

5.7.8   Parallel runs and trial runs

Migration is an exciting and risky route. Preferably, one wants to see everything running in the new service before the definitive switch is made. A test measure for this is a trial run, in which a production-like scenario is enacted with users who go through the business processes on the new service. The service will not be live, but it will be loaded with converted data. An even more thorough option is running the original systems and the service in parallel (parallel runs).

Trial runs and parallel runs are very expensive. With a trial run, two environments are needed, and end users need to use the two systems in parallel. The input can be duplicated automatically by means of a continuous migration, conversion, or data synchronization from the original (live) systems to the (parallel) service. The advantage of the cloud is that the environment does not need to be paid for separately: it is delivered with the service. That makes it cheaper to add a trial run phase or parallel run phase in the migration to the cloud.

An important factor in trial/parallel runs is determining which criteria are the basis for making the switch and turning the service on. The test manager has an important role in this determination: putting together a go-live report. Consider the following suggestions for go-live criteria based on the trial/parallel run:

■ There are no blocking issues from the parallel process.
■ The service delivers the same results as the original systems (when there are differences, they need to be explained).
■ The parallel processes are free from failure for a predefined amount of time.
■ A representative set of business processes is running in a parallel process.

There is a lot of effort needed to keep the parallel process running. Therefore, the service must be tested beforehand to make sure it works properly.

5.8   Testing due to legislation and regulations

An organization needs to take legislation and regulations into account when configuring the IT landscape. The use of services is complicated by the legislation aimed at different industries, such as legislation with regard to financial accountability (the Sarbanes–Oxley Act is an example), pharmaceuticals, medical care, and telecoms. The application of most legislation and regulations does not change substantially when services are in the cloud, but demonstrating conformity is not getting easier. This section mainly targets the legislation and regulations that are codependent with the location and protection of data that is brought to the cloud. It is about which requirements apply and not how they are being complied with by putting security measures in place.

Other legal matters are warrantee conditions, liabilities, and the contract between customer and supplier. These legal issues are outside the scope of this section.

When data that is subject to privacy legislation is migrated to a service for storage or processing, other parties potentially get access to it. With cross-border data traffic in the cloud, another factor is added: multiple laws and regulations for each of the countries involved. Legislation can hardly keep up with developments in the IT world. And cloud computing is, for the most part, in the pioneer phase.

For the tester, legislation and regulations are a form of test basis. It is critical to list all applicable legislation and regulations. This inventory potentially brings a number of problems to light, such as contradictory legislation from different countries. Then the intended service is tested to determine whether the rules can be met. In this specialized field, the tester and the legal representative need to complement each other.

What is to be done when issues arise? These are not often matters that can be solved with a software fix. In practice, a compromise has to be made, possibly by not complying with all the rules. This is in anticipation of the movement of international legislation and regulations to better fit the new technology advances that cloud computing offers. Of course, the tester or test manager does not make this decision, but they advise, together with a lawyer, the managers that are empowered to make decisions.

5.8.1 Inventory of legislation and regulations

Most countries have laws or rules for the way in which data needs to be handled, such as where it is held (in the world), how long it is held, how it is processed, and how it is accessed. The interests of the people to whom the data is connected are key in all cases. For a company, this can be the end users of the service, but, for instance, it may also be employees of the company for which personnel data is stored or processed in the cloud.

Privacy legislation

For recent details on the current legislation, one has to seek legal sources. In the Netherlands, legislation exists that puts limitations on the handling of personal data, and there is related European legislation. There are national (Dutch Data Protection Authority) and European (European Data Protection Supervisor) organizations that check for the correct application of the rules.

Here are some examples of privacy laws:

- Dutch Data Protection Act
- EU Directive 95/46/EC on the protection of personal data
- US-EU Safe Harbor

Data location

In a legal context, the world is divided into locations where data can and cannot be stored without problems. It is important to determine where these borders lie. For the Netherlands, many European and several other countries lie within these borders. The service needs to be investigated to determine where the data will be held. This seems contradictory to the cloud's *raison d'être* (the customer really wouldn't want to have that responsibility), but the law requires that the data owner is responsible for ensuring that the protection of personal data is at the required level wherever it is held.

In the search for the routes and locations of the data, several complicating issues can be encountered. For instance, services often are stacked, such as a SaaS supplier that uses a PaaS supplier, who in turn bases the service on the infrastructure from another supplier. It is the IaaS that determines the physical location of the data. In addition to the physical location of the data storage, the office locations of the different suppliers might be relevant: when they fall under different jurisdictions, the diversity of laws and rules increases even further.

Service suppliers continuously search for new opportunities for expansion and for lowering costs. That is why suppliers move the physical locations of the service software and, as a result, the location of the data. Based on supply and demand, a market in data storage can even arise: moving data to the most cost-effective location. The customer is not inconvenienced and may not even know about it.

Another aspect of the cloud is that data is not always in one location but spread over different places. To comply with the high-availability requirements, the data is kept up to date in the different locations through synchronization. Users contribute to this multi-location scenario: the mailbox in the cloud synchronizes with the laptop at work, the PC at home, and the tablet, not to mention the smartphone on the road. In short, finding an answer to the question, "Where is my data?" is far from trivial.

There are a number of possible outcomes to an investigation into the location of data in the cloud:

- There is nothing, or hardly anything, to be found on this subject; this might be a reason not to start using the service and to choose a service where the location is documented (or for now, completely renounce cloud computing).

- The service stores data outside the borders of permitted countries and the service cannot be used immediately, but with additional measures it may become possible.
- The service stores data within the borders of permitted counties. When business-critical data is involved, additional guarantees might be needed about the location and access to data, captured in a contract between the customer and supplier (for instance, the possibility of performing audits at the service supplier).

Additional agreements

Without going into detail on all the legal ins and outs, it can be stated that the customer of the service will always and everywhere have the final responsibility for controlling the privacy interests of the people to whom the data is related. Standard procedures for offering data for processing or storing outside the borders of permitted countries may be available from official bodies that monitor the protection of personal data. The most important requirement is that the protection level "travels" with the data, wherever it is. The customer of the service needs control over it, with additional agreements along the entire route the data follows. The person responsible for the data is not only accountable to the legislator, but also to the people whose personal data is moved; they need to be informed.

International operating companies have the opportunity to create so-called "binding corporate rules": company locations outside the European Union (EU) comply with the same privacy rules as within the EU. Service suppliers could use these same rules.

Other legislation

Privacy legislation covers individuals. There are also other stakeholders around data storage. Financial regulations, for instance, contain provisions for retention periods and banking secrecy. Some sectors have to do with professional secrecy (such as health care). Other sources of legislation with regard to administrative organizations are civil codes, and fiscal laws. The (international) government is increasingly imposing requirements on tracing and temporarily storing Internet traffic for investigating criminal and terrorist activity.

Other obligations

A customer has, by using services, outsourced certain matters. A part of the customer's process runs externally and the customer's control over it is limited. It is recommended that customers analyze in advance the extent to which they can meet their obligations when the service is not available (through bankruptcy, business conflict, or failure).

Investigation is needed to determine whether customers who use licensed software are permitted to use it in the cloud.

Conflicting laws and rules

It can be that in the different countries where the data ends up, conflicting requirements are in place, for instance with regard to the retention period: in one country data may need to be retained a minimum of five years and in another a maximum of three years. These cannot be easily reconciled. The accompanying risks need to be assessed; where it seems logical, choose the legislation in the home country as a starting point.

Impending laws and rules

In addition to complying with the regulations in countries in which data is processed or stored, there is another reason for analyzing local legislation. There can be legislation by which the local government can gain control over the data (the best known example is the Patriot Act: the American government can enforce access to data in the case of a suspected terrorist threat). This is a risk for the customer's intellectual capital (and, in fact, also for the service supplier's).

There can also be cases of unreliable governments: countries with low IT cost structures are sometimes less transparently organized. This represents a hard-to-grasp risk that needs to be weighed when choosing to use services from a supplier or when a supplier rolls out services in such countries.

5.8.2   Checking for legislation and regulations

Which instruments can the test manager implement to check the service for legislation and regulations?

- Provide help in listing the data that is stored in the cloud and the requirements that are applicable to this data is an important step in itself: senior people in the organization are made aware of the requirements and risks and make a conscious choice of a service (or decide not to). In this phase, legal support is necessary when risks are medium or high.
- Provide help in listing the supplier terms and checking whether they are contradictory to the customer's requirements.

  Example. A supplier of a storage service claims to be the owner of the intellectual capital of all data stored at their facilities. It is highly unlikely that this is compatible with the interests of the organization that is the actual owner of the data.

- When risks are high, an audit can be performed. Performing an audit is something that requires specialists, which in most cases have to be found outside the organization.
- When all risks and possible bottlenecks are known, senior management needs to make the decision, partly based on the test manager's advice, whether this service can be used in the organization or not.
- Testing and checking data security is, as always, fundamental.

5.9 Testing in production

In traditional development projects, a support department is present that takes over responsibility for the software after it is implemented in production. Patches, changes, and so on are tested and rolled out by the support department. The supplier maintains the services, so the customer doesn't need a support department for the maintenance of the service itself. Despite the savings that can be achieved, this poses a problem because test activities still need to be done with and around the service. It seems obvious that the test manager, as in the implementation phase, has this responsibility.

In addition, it is important to determine whether the supplier keeps their promises with regard to nonfunctional attributes, such as availability and performance. Testing, the use of monitoring tools, and logging are the appointed measures.

5.9.1 Continuity in production in the case of changes

The service and the service's environment are continuously subject to change (see Figure 5–22). After a successful implementation, continuity is constantly threatened. A number of these changes are described next.

Changes in the service

Suppliers, for different reasons, make changes to the service. Some of these reasons include to solve problems, for improvements, in anticipation of growth, to replace infrastructure, to apply security updates, and to process change requests from customers. In certain cases this will be announced, and perhaps the option is offered to test the changed version. More often, customers are confronted with updates after they are implemented. Not all changes are communicated to customers. There are, therefore, three scenarios, each with a specific test approach:

- **Announced changes**. Organize a test that targets the changes and perform an E2E regression test on the high-risk parts of the service.
- **Retrospective information about changes**. Organize a test that targets the changes and perform an E2E regression test on the high-risk parts of the service.
- **No information**. Limit the risk by regularly performing the E2E regression tests on the parts with the highest risk.

Although a service can be tested alone, an E2E test is preferable for testing continuity. See section 3.1.3 for more information on putting together and executing E2E tests.

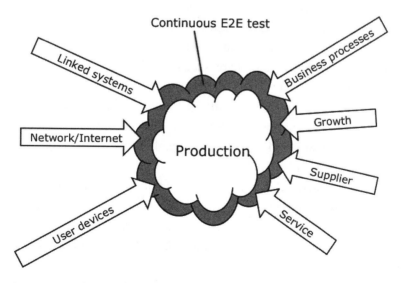

Figure 5–22   *Everything changes*

Changes in other systems

When the service is connected to other systems, the E2E functionality may be threatened when changes occur in these systems. Normally, these changes do not come as a surprise because the systems concerned are in maintenance and under the customer's control. A regression test, targeting the changes, in combination with an E2E regression test should be in place. When there are changes in the interfaces, a specific test for the interfaces between the service and the changed systems is also needed.

An interesting and obvious change in other systems is that they are increasingly brought into the cloud.

Changes at the supplier

In this instance, we are not referring to the service itself that is changed but other changes that can affect the service, such as changes in the invoicing model, takeover of the service ownership by another party, opening new locations to support to the service, and changes to the website to which more or less capacity can be configured. The changes introduce risks for continuity in the (near) future.

A measure to be used here is reevaluating the supplier against the selection criteria. By checking whether things have changed, you can determine the appropriateness of continuing with the same supplier. Running through the selection process with a certain amount of regularity (for instance, yearly) is a good strategy to track changes. Because the cloud computing market is continuously changing and developing, there is a chance that when evaluating selection criteria, a more suitable supplier is on the market. Switching to such a supplier should be seriously considered. This will require a structured approach to secure continuity during the transfer. It can be expected that switching from supplier A to supplier B will become increasingly easier in the future, helped by increasing standardization.

With the chaotic development in the world of cloud computing, it can happen that successful suppliers grow strongly, and as a result, the match between the customer and supplier is lost (see Figure 5–23). A previous personal understanding becomes professional and distant. A relatively small customer can be at the mercy of a larger supplier. On the other hand, the professionalization of a service supplier might result in a better match for the customer's needs.

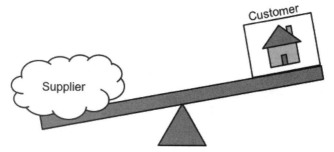

Figure 5–23 *Balance between supplier and customer*

Changes in the business processes

Change can also occur on the customer side. It is possible that the set of requirements that was used as a basis for choosing a service changes in such a way that evaluating the selection criteria leads to choosing another service. In that case, the implementation process needs to be run through again from the start. Changes can also be less radical and just lead to a change in the way the service is used. The E2E test cases will need to be adjusted to take into account the new procedures and preferably executed prior to implementing the changes. In section 5.6, the testing of the business processes in combination with the service is discussed in more detail.

Growth

An important strength of cloud computing is the option to scale service capacity to match the need. Nonetheless, in practice, there are certain bandwidths within which growth can be accommodated. Growth also needs to be considered in relation to the supplier. It is very likely that a supplier is suitable for small volumes but that other suppliers can provide the service with better terms as the volume grows. Measuring the amount of use on a regular basis, comparing this to expectations, and reconsidering the selection criteria are important measures to manage risks. Note that the entire use is not generated from within the walls of the organization. With the New World of Work and increasing use of mobile resources, use also is generated at other locations and times.

Changes in connected resources

A thin client contains software such as an operating system and a browser. These are regularly updated, if only to keep up with security updates. Problems that may arise in the interaction with the service can be tested in a test environment with an E2E test. This, of course, also goes for changes in other components, such as firewalls, load balancers, and routers. It is more difficult to anticipate changes in mobile devices and what devices the users may have in the future (BYOD). In most cases, versions and updates to these devices cannot be overseen. The users have to find out for themselves to a certain extent. One can choose to include a selection of frequently used resources with up-to-date software versions in the E2E regression test. Assuming that users keep their devices up to date, continuity will be reasonably secured.

Changes to the Internet

Although the Internet is generally seen as a transparent medium, in reality it is a large, complicated machine that is continuously being developed. The Internet contains a lot of functionality, such as addressing, routing, caching, and data traffic security. The behavior of the data in the Internet is translated into the cloud. The broad network access characteristic of cloud computing is directly dependent on the proper functioning of the Internet. Many changes in the Internet are not immediately visible or known to the customer or service supplier. A regularly run E2E regression test is a measure that, unfortunately in hindsight, can detect if something has changed in the Internet connection and whether the change has an impact on the use of the service. There are also changes in the Internet that can be expected, such as the implementation of IPv6. When problems with the Internet disrupt the functioning of the service, it will lead to an issue in the E2E test setup.

Conclusion

In conclusion, it can be stated that the test manager needs to be attentive to all possible changes in the operational stage. Thought needs to be given to matters that can disrupt the continuity of the service and, with that, the business process. In addition, the test manager needs to actively initiate measures and check with sufficient regularity to determine whether continuity is threatened by changes that are off the radar.

5.9.2   Measuring guarantees

An advantage of cloud computing is the pay-per-use principle. Only what is used is paid for. That leads to the following questions for the customer: Do I get what I pay for? Do I pay too much? With large customers, a lot of money and a large vested interest are involved, so it is worth finding good answers to these two questions. It is about evaluating the contract agreements on the basis of guaranteed or agreed KPIs. In Chapter 3, reaching agreement with the supplier is discussed. A number of obvious KPIs for services and measuring the levels achieved in production are discussed next.

Availability

Suppliers advertise with high service availability percentages. In most cases they consist of three or more nines (>99.9 percent), but 100 percent is also advertised. A number of comments may be made about the availability percentage. 99.9 percent availability in a year, for instance, means that a service with a disruption of over eight hours per year complies with the terms of the guarantee. This can mean the loss of a day's worth of revenues. In addition, the supplier may exclude certain periods from availability measuring (for instance, for maintenance periods). This can shed another light on the theoretically high availability percentages. For a customer, it is important to establish which availability periods really matter. When the stakes (risk) are high enough, a customer can decide to measure actual availability.

Availability can be measured with the help of monitoring tools that observe whether the service is interrupted. Registering failure notices is an alternative approach. At the end of each period, it can be established whether the service's availability has reached the required level.

It is possible that the supplier monitors availability for each customer or service. When it is shown in practice that this is sufficiently reliable, the customer has no need to do this monitoring, which, in turn, results in savings.

Performance

For performance the same comments about availability are, to some extent, applicable. Performance guarantees for user applications are usually given within certain margins, such as "response time in 95 percent of cases within x seconds." Just as with availability, it is important to find out how this relates to the desired performance during peaks and troughs, different weekdays, periods during the year, and so on. In other words, does the customer experience the performance guaranteed by the supplier when it is needed, and is the guaranteed performance sufficient for continuity in production? In addition to KPIs for response times, there are other performance-related KPIs, such as upload, download, and synchronization speeds. Often these are configurable and sometimes they are dynamic in nature, such as an upload speed that is a maximum of 75 percent of the actual bandwidth. As a result, other customers can seriously affect performance.

To evaluate the performance in production, the following needs to be clear:

- Which performance KPIs are important enough to measure
- Which guarantees the supplier provides
- How the KPIs can be measured

Section 5.2 explained how the testing of performance works. In measuring performance, it is important to be able to determine the bottlenecks and what and where to measure to be able to find them. There are many options: the customer's resources, the network, the in-house software (with PaaS and IaaS), or the supplier's software. Just as with availability, evaluation can be based on measurement or based on complaints.

Scalability

By measuring availability and performance, value for money can be determined. At the same time, scalability is tested.

How can it be determined whether there is too much capacity? If this is the case, it needs to be scaled down to reduce expenditure on the service. To the extent where the capacity used can be calculated, this is quite easy to assess. For instance, if 50 of a possible 100 mailboxes are in use, probably a smaller package can be used. By keeping track of actual use of the service in production, money can be saved. Services will increasingly offer the option of showing the capacity used.

Security

What is a suitable KPI for security? How can you measure security? One way to do this is by collecting security issues, but that does not provide a comfortable feeling. The risk of failure for security issues is too high to use this as a metric.

The level of security needs to be measured actively. Section 5.3 describes how security can be tested.

Reading log files and audit trails, where it can be seen which user at what time had access to which information, is a method that can be easily accomplished in production. Other security checks, such as audits and penetration tests, are cumbersome to apply often. However, these tests should be periodically run, perhaps yearly.

One approach is to take the following steps:

1. List which security measures in production need to be monitored (risk based).
2. Determine measuring method and frequency.
3. Evaluate the results.

The objective is to assess the quality of the defense line and locate weak spots. It is also important that the customer's expectations match the security guaranteed by the supplier.

5.9.3   Original selection criteria evaluation

Once a service has been chosen, implemented, and used in production, it appears that the threshold to reevaluate the selection criteria against the service on a regular basis is quite unlikely. It is recommended that, on a yearly basis, it is determined whether there are any new, more favorable options available. Changes in the current service, the IT environment it is part of, and the business processes can lead to a reevaluation of the chosen approach. In addition, it can just be that with the chaotic development of cloud computing, new services are developed and offered that give rise to the requirement to switch.

Comparing the current service solution with new alternatives is done in the same way as with the original selection; see section 5.1.

Here are the most important triggers for a service selection evaluation:

- Significant issues with the current solution
- Significant changes coming up with the service or service supplier that can have a negative impact
- Significant changes in the business processes
- Availability of new or better services or services with more favorable terms

A migration to another service is, of course, not free. With a possible switch to a new service, the business case needs to be properly evaluated.

5.9.4   Practical points to note

(E2E) Regression test

An important instrument for testing in production is the E2E regression test. The business processes are tested to establish whether they still run properly. Depending on the frequency of changes (in certain environments patches are rolled out daily, so this could also happen with a service), a daily regression test can be needed. In section 3.1.3 more detailed attention is paid to setting up an E2E test. An E2E regression test is complex and relatively expensive. When issues in a particular area—for example, integration between the service and one particular system—are found on a regular basis during the E2E test, a more local regression test can be considered as an addition. This would not require the E2E test to be deployed every time, which can lead to savings.

Measurement methods for KPIs

When the customer is complaining to the supplier about not meeting a guaranteed KPI, the measurement method can be subject to fierce debate. This is prevented by recording the measurement method in the SLA in advance.

6 Completion

How can a book that is about something that still needs to reach full development be concluded? For starters, by establishing that practice will show to what extent the test measures fit and which further innovations are needed. More risks will undoubtedly be identified, existing risks will reveal to be less relevant than imagined, and the test measures will be adjusted accordingly. Further developments will be followed and various media additions to this book will appear. *Testing Cloud Services* offers the entire approach, from identifying risks to taking test measures.

With all the risks and test measures that are described in this book, the impression might be that going to the cloud is fairly risky. In other words, if this needs to be tested so extensively, is cloud computing such a good idea? But here the universal rule is valid:

No Risk, No Test

Example. Based on the extent of the security risks, one can choose from the following options:

- **Not test at all.** *This is valid for widely used and proven services such as email.*
- **Hiring a test company.** *This is advisable when the business stands or falls on proper functioning and/or it is plausible that malicious parties will try to gain access to company data.*
- **Test in-house.** *All other cases.*

With the use of the approach in this book, the test manager can put together a generic test strategy that applies to the organization's context. Certain risks are, for instance, general and apply to every service that is introduced into the organization's IT landscape. Choices are made by each organization. Certain test measures will become a permanent part of the test strategies for services in the cloud, such as setting up a continuous E2E regression test.

The good news for the test manager is that cloud computing offers plenty of opportunities. Broadening the role of the test manager fits in with the IT profession becoming more mature: the shift from "Do I get what is promised and are there no errors in it?" to "Is this a correctly functioning solution for the organization?" This requires involvement in all phases of the entire life cycle of providing IT services from the cloud. In addition, it also requires more knowledge in the field of testing nonfunctional requirements. The key is to select the tools that fit the context.

This book is just the beginning of testing of and with services in the cloud: the warm-up is finished, but the match still needs to be played!

Glossary

Term	Definition
ADSL	Method for data transfer over a cable.
audit trail	Capturing information to enable the history of a transaction to be viewed.
CDMI	Cloud Data Management Interface: functional interface that allows applications to interact with the cloud for data storage.
checksum	Method to verify that no errors have arisen in the data transmission. Performed mathematically.
DDoS	Distributed Denial of Service is an attack where multiple systems target a single system with the aim of taking it out of service.
driver	Software with limited functionality that enables the tester to send data to the test object. This software replaces a system that normally would supply this information, but which is not (yet) present.
DTAP	Develop–test–acceptance–production environment: term to indicate that developers, (system) testers and acceptance testers each have their own adequate environments in which to do their tasks without disruption from the others.
EDGE	A service for delivering data to mobiles.
GPRS	A service for delivering data to mobiles.
HTTP	Hypertext Transfer Protocol is a protocol used for exchanging documents on the Internet.
IPv6 (and IPv4)	Internet addresses. IPv4 (old) uses addresses of 32 bits and IPv6 (new) uses addresses of 128 bits.
JSON	JavaScript Object Notation is a text-based open standard designed for human-readable data interchange. Javascript is a programming language used in websites.
KPI	Key performance indicators are used to evaluate success, or to evaluate the success of particular activities. KPIs are included in contracts between organizations.
load balancer	A load balancer distributes workload across multiple computers or other resources. The objective is to prevent overload and to achieve better performance.
mock	Software with limited functionality that enables the tester to send data to the test object, after receiving data from the test object. This software replaces a system that normally would receive and send the data, but is not (yet) present.

MUSA	See *Software Reliability Engineering*, 2nd edition, John D. Musa, Author-house, ISBN 1-4184-9387-2.
OCCI	Open Cloud Computing Interface is an interface that initially was meant to remotely manage IaaS. Today it is also applicable to PaaS and SaaS (http://occi-wg.org/).
ODF	Open Document Format: a standard for document exchange.
OVF	Open Virtualization Format: a standard for interoperability of virtual environments.
POC	A proof of concept is a basic implementation to demonstrate that the proposed solution is going to work.
process cycle test	See *TMap Next, for Result-driven Testing*, Tim Koomen et al., UTN Publishers, ISBN 90-72194-79-4.
real life test	See *TMap Next, for Result-driven Testing*, Tim Koomen et al., UTN Publishers, ISBN 90-72194-79-4.
REST	Representational State Transfer: an architectural style for systems such as the World Wide Web.
sandbox	A sandbox is a safe environment in which to experiment.
SBTM	Session-based test management: http://www.satisfice.com/articles/sbtm.pdf.
SLA	Service level agreement: a documented agreement between a supplier and customer.
SOAP	Simple Object Access Protocol: a widely used protocol, including on the Internet.
SSL	Secure Sockets Layer: a system to protect certain types of messages on the Internet.
SSO	Single Sign On: a method to allow a user to perform tasks in multiple systems after logging into an information system, where this system serves as an authentication source for the other systems.
staging	A method in which website content is placed in a test environment before publication in order to test and, if necessary, modify the content and appearance.
stub	Software with limited functionality that enables the tester to receive data from the test object. This software replaces a system that normally would send the data, but is not (yet) present.
thin client	A small (thin) computer that servers as a customer (client) of a large, central computer, where the majority of the processing takes place.
TLS	Transport Layer Security: mechanism used for certain types of messaging over the Internet.
TMap	See *TMap Next, for Result-driven Testing*, Tim Koomen et al., UTN Publishers, ISBN 90-72194-79-4.
TMMi	A method for determining the maturity of testing processes.
TOGA	Test Outsourcing Government Approach: an approach for the successful outsourcing of testing activities. See http://www.polteq.com/en/.
TPI	Test Process Improvement: see *TPI Next, Business Driven Test Process Improvement*, Sogeti, UTN Publishers, ISBN 90-72194-97-7.
VPN	Virtual private network: a method by which a local network is made accessible on the Internet.

W3C	World Wide Web Consortium: see http://www.w3.org.
WEP	Wired Equivalent Privacy: an outdated wireless security method.
WPA	Wi-Fi Protected Access: Wi-Fi security method.
WSDL	The Web Services Description Language is an XML-based interface description language that is used for describing the functionality offered by a web service.
XML	eXtensible Markup Language: a language used to store data in a structured way.

Index